GOD:

A GOOD FATHER

GOD:

A GOOD FATHER

Michael Phillips

Destiny Image® Publishers, Inc.
P.O. Box 310
Shippensburg, PA 17257-0310

"Speaking to the Purposes of God for This Generation
and for the Generations to Come"

ISBN 0-7684-2123-3
Library of Congress Catalog Card Number 2001-132713

For Worldwide Distribution
Printed in the U.S.A.

This book and all other Destiny Image, Revival Press,
MercyPlace, Fresh Bread, Destiny Image Fiction,
and Treasure House books are available
at Christian bookstores and distributors worldwide.

For a U.S. bookstore nearest you, call **1-800-722-6774**.
For more information on foreign distributors, call **717-532-3040**.
Or reach us on the Internet: **www.destinyimage.com**

THIS IS AND HAS BEEN THE FATHER'S WORK
FROM THE BEGINNING—TO BRING US
INTO THE HOME OF HIS HEART.

—GEORGE MACDONALD

CONTENTS

INTRODUCTION

I WOULD LIKE TO INVITE YOU ON A JOURNEY, an inner quest out of the valleys and low places of our spiritual abodes to the high mountains.

It is usually more comfortable to remain lower down the slopes where crowds of the like-minded congregate. The doctrines and traditions there are familiar and unthreatening. It takes little courage to go through the same motions and discuss the same principles of seeming spirituality week after week...year after year.

But there's not much challenge...not much to be seen from the valleys and foothills. A rote religion offers endless repetition, but little vibrancy. And if one is content thus, with the ruts and routines of valley life, he or she will not find this pilgrimage of much interest. But for you men and women who desire something more, I invite you to join an adventure that will lead to wider vistas and broader outlooks than are possible from the lowlands.

As we journey together, we will probe into areas and be challenged to reflect on some things that the elders and theologians of the low cities don't like their inhabitants thinking about. But bold, prayerfully imaginative faith is necessary if a Christian life is to remain fresh and progress toward intimacy with God. It takes honest, vigorous thought to get above the fogs that cover much of these lower regions with traditional but unsatisfying explanations of God and His ways.

I say this so that you will know what kind of book this is. If you are looking for a concise list of x-number of things you can go out and do tomorrow to achieve intimacy with God, you have picked up the wrong book. This is no how-to manual—no twelve-steps-to-this and ten-steps-to-that and four-easy-methods-toward-that. As I made clear several years ago in the volume entitled *A God to Call Father*, of which this is a new, revised, and updated edition, this is a book about *ideas*.

I am going to challenge you instead to *think* differently about God and how you relate yourself to Him. Clearly, it is impossible to know God, to obey Him, to function within His family, or to understand His Word if we are thinking incorrectly about who He Himself is.

Practicality is a worthwhile and necessary priority. However, it is only half the life equation. Here we will attempt to construct a foundation, a way of viewing God, upon which the practicalities of life can be built. We will be orienting our beliefs and attitudes in some new directions concerning just exactly who God is.

Much of our thinking about Him is rooted in teachings, traditions, and principles we have been taught and impressions we have gleaned from others, rather than from having prayed our way through certain important scriptural concepts for ourselves.

Our knowing of God, therefore, is sketchy, hazy, and incomplete.

That is what we will do here together—learn to think in fresh, invigorating, and liberating new ways, about He whom Jesus called our *Father*.

There will certainly be a *do* involved—the very important exercise of learning to relate ourselves to the Father in the exciting ways in which Jesus walked with Him and invited us to do likewise. But it will be a "do" measured, not with hands, fingers, and feet...but rather with brains and hearts.

We must learn to *think* rightly about God. Until that foundation has been laid, nothing else will make much sense.

Now I hope you may come to view this as one of the most practical books you ever read. But not because you were given a list of points to memorize, or because you took notes or underlined various clever passages, but rather because the ideas we explore prompt you to go outside alone and gaze upward toward the mountaintops of your faith, and say, *"Oh, God, teach me to think rightly about You. Help me know You more intimately as my very personal Father."*

Michael Phillips
Eureka, California

1

THE INSTINCT TO LOOK UP

DEEP WITHIN EVERY MORTAL HEART LIES A CREATED HUNGER for the heavenly mountains of God's presence.

All of us, from our infancy, have silently wondered what lies on the slopes above the mists, hidden from view...up where God dwells.

The animal kingdom comes into existence looking abroad upon the land. Those of the species known as mankind, however, enter life with their gaze directed *upward*.

Lower forms of life are born with *physical* instincts. Their impulses operate *horizontally*, telling them intuitively how to relate to the world around them, to others of their genus, and to different species. Theirs is an instinct toward procreation and survival, toward horizontal relationship and existence.

Man, however, created in the image of God, possesses instincts of an altogether different nature. Within us the Creator has implanted *spiritual* instincts, tending far beyond mere physical survival. Impulses akin to animal instincts constantly surface within us and are certainly intrinsic to our make-up, but they remain secondary to the deepest nature of human personhood.

Man's instinct is *vertical*—a yearning after the high, the lasting, the eternal. It is an instinct after growth, after betterment, after significance, after something and Someone above us. When in touch with the truest regions of our humanness, we seek the sky, not the earth.

1

The lungs of our soul ache to breathe the air of eternity. And though mists obscure our sight, our deepest perceptions tell us there is more to existence than that which our physical eyes see around us. Something affirms to our innermost being that there are *higher* regions where we might live, where the air is cleaner, where vision is keener, where the senses come more fully *alive*.

A divine restlessness exists within the innermost chambers of our soul, stirring us with longings we cannot identify, which we futilely attempt to satisfy with bread that is not food, made from husks that are not grain.

The mountains beckon us who live in the valley. Our deepest selves are out of step with the modern life pushing and shoving us on every side. You have caught yourself, as have I, glancing upward, though you may not even know what it is your heart seeks.

> THE LUNGS OF OUR SOUL ACHE TO BREATHE THE AIR OF ETERNITY.

Before the valley philosophers and theologians created the mists with their self-contradictory babblings, there were voices among us, calling us to heed that instinctive longing.

Augustine, that ancient and venerable saint, maintained that "the heart of man is restless until it finds its rest"[1] in Him.

Thomas Kelly, that recent and venerable saint, called it "the Light within."[2]

Blaise Pascal, that seventeenth-century defender of the faith, defined it as a God-shaped vacuum, an "infinite abyss," which "can be filled only with an infinite and immutable object...God himself."

Hannah Hurnard, that pioneer of mountain byways, wrote of life on the "high places."[3]

And George MacDonald, that nineteenth-century spiritual sage who saw high beyond the mists, said, "This is and has been the Father's work from the beginning—to bring us into the home of his heart. This is our destiny."[4]

Why, then, do so few discover the shape of that vacuum in their souls, the illumination of that Light residing within?

Why do so many of us resist the challenge to climb to the mountaintops?

Why is the home of God's heart so remote from where we live out our days? Why do we go to our graves with that destiny, that high calling, unfulfilled? Why is the human species so at odds with this inborn instinct of his nature?

Allow me to offer three reasons.

One, unlike the animals, man has been given *choice*.

We share instinct with the animal kingdom, but ours has this difference— we may ignore it. Animals can be no other than they are. Their instinct defines their essence. Not so man. Man may, or may not, follow his instincts, for he has been provided an internal on-off switch that regulates the very centers of his being: the *mind*, where intellect develops; the *heart*, where emotions blossom; and the *soul*, where spiritual sensitivities ripen.

This switch, which controls each of the above, is located in that most decisive of regions: the *will*.

The switch is called *choice*.

The degree to which man *chooses* to follow his inborn, God-hungry instinct will determine the extent to which mind, heart, and soul reach their fullness of maturity and potential, and whether they operate with unity and harmony inside him.

Two, many factors of modern society work strenuously to dull the inner Voice that speaks of the Light, calling us toward that true and only destination where our mind, heart, soul, and will can find rest, peace, and totality of being.

Contemporary society and our practical peers of modernism tell us, "There is nothing out there." We may gaze upward all we want, they say, but we will find nothing but blue emptiness. There are no heavenly peaks surrounding this valley where man must dwell.

3

Indeed, they say, we must look *within* if we would discover the signif-icance we seek. *Man himself* is the emphatic and only center of the universe.

Three, sin, as intrinsic to the human disposition as the intuitive upward bent of our inner sight, declares, as it has since the days of the Garden, that there is no one to whom we *must* look up, no one to whom we *owe* alle-giance. This lie from sin's smooth lips grates contrary to our deepest intu-ition. Deep down, we *know* differently, yet it is a lie our lower nature eagerly receives.

You, and no one else, says the enemy, are the sole master of your fate. No one has the right to exact obedience from you. You have no need of any Other. There exists no injunction to bow before a God, a Creator, a Lord.

The lie is *independence*. It comes from the lowest bowels of the earth, not the high realms of the heavenly mountains.

Instinct calls upward. *The lie* forces our gaze downward. In believing it, we fight against our very self.

Choice, modernism, and sin prevent us from apprehending our destiny and keep us from the destination and mountaintop sanctuary wherein we were made to dwell.

ENDNOTES

1. St. Augustine of Hippo, *Confessions*, Book 1, opening prayer.
2. Thomas Kelly, *A Testament of Devotion* (New York: Harper & Row, 1941), p. 29.
3. Hannah Hurnard, *Hinds' Feet on High Places* (C.L.C., 1955), no page.
4. George MacDonald, *Unspoken Sermons*, Second Series (London: Longmans, Green, & Co., 1885), p. 261.

2

MODERNISM RESENTS
FATHERHOOD

Does not your heart leap at the thought of a home for your innermost spirit, sheltered from the anxieties that press upon you daily?

Do you not long, in your quiet moments, for relief from the restlessness and frustration with which life seems filled? Would you not rejoice to find that you might enter into a center of calm, where the intensities of today's frantic pace lose their power to make you tense and anxious?

Consider, my hearers, the waters of a deep quiet pool within you, whose calm surface the pressuring stones of life cannot disturb. Does not the thought of such a place cause you to sigh, "Ah, could such truly be possible...for me? Could such waters—refreshing and cold and invigorating—quench my every thirst, always renewing themselves, never running dry?"

The place from which such waters bubble forth is neither unattainable nor distant. To reach it will take a climb, it is true. And it is no quest for the faint of heart.

Up there, in the mountains, waters stream forth from divine springs. It only remains for you to find the source of those emerald headwaters, and then bend down to drink.

"But be practical," say a thousand voices at once. "Life is to be lived in the here and now. Whoever said we were supposed to be saints? You don't want to turn into a nun, a preacher, a monk, a mystic!"

Multitudinous and persistent will be the bombarding objections, even from your Christian friends living their Christian lives in their foothill communities.

All your training, all of what you consider the "practical experience" of your life, all your concerns over that most harmless demon called "what other people might think," all the observations of your friends and acquaintances and how *they* live their lives in the low places, all your anxieties about turning into a stuffy cleric...all these will bring their arguments to bear against you in denial of the Voice calling you to look upward and inward. Forget about it, they will tell you, and get on with *real* life.

Yet their arguments collide with disconsonance against that instinct you cannot hide from, that *you-est* part of you—the urge that says there *is* more than these so-called practicalities would admit.

The collision between sky-gazing intuition and earthbound reasoning is exacerbated all the more when we mention *fatherhood* as the source of this higher destination, the divine Headwaters of the high-mountain spring. For the word *father* itself has become odious to modern ears.

Attempting to disrupt the inner summons from on high, discrepant voices pressure and persuade us to reject the concept of fatherhood in three of its essential attributes:

—Its *masculinity*,

—Its *authority*,

—Its *God-ness*.

An enshrouding cloud has settled over the valley and foothills, graying and obscuring our vision of the mountains by blocking the truths inherent in masculinity, authority, and God-ness, thus assuring our rebellion against these three inherent elements of fatherhood.

By our own *choice*, we revolt against the very notion of someone other than ourselves in *authority*.

Modern society, at every turn, prevails upon us with a thousand subtleties to reject *masculinity*.

And the *sin* to which man succumbs draws us into the lie of independence, persuading us there is no *God* to whom we owe allegiance.

Fatherhood as we have traditionally known it, say all three, is an outmoded convention from some archaic era. Times have changed, and so must our approach to this mythical thing our unenlightened predecessors called by such an oppressive name. We will keep the term, they say, but it must be utterly redefined. It must be stripped of its authority, de-masculinized, and humanized. Only then will it be unthreatening enough to suit us.

Those previously existing under the weight of its authority must be given rights of cosignificant status so that no one rules *over* any other. In this enlightened age, no child nor woman should feel lesser in rank.

Its masculinity must be given an equal injection of feminism. The genders will then be equipotent in their stature.

Moreover, they add, the Fatherhood of God must be irrevocably rejected for the illusionary absurdity it always was. It is to God's *Person*ness we must look, giving femininity and motherhood their equal share with the former bias of *His*ness.

Thus, these valley corruptions of antifatherhood enter our perceptions at all levels, carrying out their cancerous work, eating away the very marrow of our spiritual fiber.

ANTIFATHERHOOD IS NO BENIGN CANCER; IT IS THE FATAL MALIGNANCY OF MODERNISM.

Antifatherhood is no benign cancer; it is the fatal malignancy of modernism. Its curse cannot be escaped. Its molecules swirl about in the very air we breathe, and none is immune. Nor can its cells be isolated to a few remote and inconsequential regions within us where they can be "tolerated."

Antifatherhood is positively lethal. If allowed to take hold and grow, it will infect mind, heart, soul, and will with its poison. It deadens those unfamiliar with the ways of God—those who would not call themselves active "Christians"—to the very instinct that can lead them out of the quagmire of self-satisfaction, pride, despair, emptiness, and frustration.

Perhaps even more importantly, this antipathy toward fatherhood prevents those acquainted with God's work—those who *would* number themselves among the followers of Christ—from laying hold of the fullness of their childship.

Ultimately it will kill the ability of both Christians and non-Christians to *think* accurately, to *feel* appropriately, to *grow* maturely, and to *choose* wisely.

It is in that region where spiritual sensitivities sprout and grow—the soul—that the death from this antifatherhood cancer comes first. Not spiritual death—what the Bible calls eternal death, damnation. Rather, it is death to the capacity to respond correctly to the One calling to us from on high.

If you would take up the quest to find those satisfying waters that can fill the inner places, if you would lay hold of that unknown Something calling you to reach higher than you previously have, the first step of preparation is this: *to lay aside whatever may predispose you to respond negatively to authority, masculinity, and to God Himself*, whether that be background, experiences, training, tendencies of prior reactions, or teachings of modernism you have adopted as your own.

Now is neither the time nor the place to argue or explain *why* you must do so, or to debate modernity's corrupted frame of reference. For the present, if you would see above the mists, you simply must lay them aside.

The malignant fog of our previous biases has to be left behind if we are going to journey out of the valley together and embark upon the upward path toward Fatherhood.

3

THE FATHER CAN BE KNOWN

IN THE SPIRITUAL AWAKENING THAT HAS TAKEN PLACE within Christendom during the last four decades, it has become customary to regard the least understood aspect of the Godhead as the Holy Spirit.

A great revival has swept through the land, reintroducing this shadowy third member of the Trinity in a widespread way.

Underlying this renaissance of Christianity's vibrancy is the foundational assumption that those calling themselves Christians are already well acquainted with the facets of God's being that go by the name *Father* and *Son.*

It may be, however, that the least apprehended of God's triune personalities is, in fact, His Fatherhood. Having been taken for granted, the knowing of God the Father has receded into the background behind a relationship with the Son and an intimacy with the Holy Spirit.

Christians speak of "walking with Jesus." Evangelicals regard salvation as based on "a personal relationship with Jesus Christ." Charismatics across the spectrum from mainline Protestant to Catholic credit a great deal of God's activity in their lives and ministries and churches to "the work of the Holy Spirit." All Christians, whatever their orientation, pray "in Jesus' name." The revivals in the 1960s were called "the Jesus movement" and "the charismatic movement," emphasizing the exciting "new" works of the Son and Spirit.

These phrases, and the assumptions to which they lead, have caused a subtle but serious error to infiltrate our attitude toward God, eroding our understanding of the gospel message, and making almost impossible a *complete* relationship with Him in all of its threefold aspects.

That error is this: the assumption that God the Father *cannot* be known with the same approachability as Son and Spirit. His holiness prevents such knowing. A veil shrouds His face. He cannot and will not coexist with sinful man. Relationship with us, as we presently exist, is contrary to His very nature. The priest must intercede on our behalf. We cannot dare presume actually to enter His solemn and holy presence.

The inevitable but false conclusion: it is impossible to know the Father with intimacy or personal immediacy.

Of all the falsehoods perpetuated by the theologies of men, this must surely be one of the most heartbreaking to God Himself. For *it is His Father's heart He desires us to know most of all*! This is where intimacy of relationship begins. The Fatherness of God provides the very foundation for both other aspects of His divine nature. Without Fatherhood there could be neither Son nor Spirit.

> IT IS HIS FATHER'S HEART HE DESIRES US TO KNOW MOST OF ALL!

The Father sent both Son and Spirit to illuminate His being precisely because He *can* be known...and He *wants* to be known.

4

WHAT DOES *FATHER* MEAN?

WHEN WE SAY, "GOD IS OUR FATHER," what do we mean?

Is *Father* merely a term of procreation, of begetting? Is *creating* all there is to the Fatherhood of God? Does our relationship to this being we cannot see extend no further than birth—both the physical and the spiritual? Does the Father of Jesus make an appearance in the opening chapters of Genesis, and then fade into the background until the great white throne of Revelation?

Alas, we live as if such is indeed the case. We resemble ungrateful children who grab a gift but then turn their backs and walk away, never expressing thanks, never even acknowledging whence the gift originated.

All men and women take *physical* life, but most offer nothing back in response to their Maker. Most do not even view it as a gift at all but as a mere fact of the natural world.

Those numbering themselves Christians receive *spiritual* life, and give back perhaps a little more, but chiefly to the Son and Spirit. They pay only cursory heed to Him out of whom both flow—the One who sustains that life of the second birth they enjoy. They approach relationship to Him as if He were ten thousand miles away and only looked in their direction when they did something wrong.

11

Thus, by lives lived virtually independent of Him—on both physical and spiritual planes—is verified the nonunderstanding we bring to the very idea of *Father*.

We bustle about in our spiritual abodes, on a first-name and familiar basis with brothers and sisters, Son and Spirit, yet think little of the Householder Himself. We regard Him with a detachment that relegates Him to the attic regions, leaving Him uninvolved in the daily goings-on of the very place of which He is the Master.

Why? Because we find it comfortable to do so.

Whatever the Son may have told us, we can't yet help being just a little afraid of the Father. We haven't yet learned what manner of Father He is.

Jesus invites us to fellowship with Him and walk beside Him. He has given commands to be followed, it is true, but He will not press the issue. Jesus says, "I obey My Father," but He will not force us to do the same. He shows us His example, but He leaves us free to choose.

The crowds came, the crowds went. The rich young ruler came, then left. Jesus did not try to convince him to change his mind. His own best friends stumbled and occasionally fell away. Yet Jesus did not coerce. He went about His business, leaving the on-off switch of their wills fully operative.

The Holy Spirit, meanwhile, is the "feel-good" third of God's being. He will pray for us when we don't know what to pray. He guides us. He gives us of His gifts. He inspires us. He leads us into truth. Jesus called Him the Comforter, and that is what He does. He soothes and consoles. He convicts and guides.

But for those few who venture, not just two-thirds of the way into God's house, but *all* the way, through the Son and Spirit into the *Father's* presence, the parameters of the relationship between Creator and created take on huge added weight.

The words of the Father are more exacting. He says, "My Son showed you His example...now you *must* obey. He left you room...I will leave you none."

He says, "When I send you My Spirit, He may give you of My pleasing gifts. But the reason is only to enable you to give your life wholly to *Me*. The gifts I, as Father, give are all good, and are even richer and more complete than what He showed you. But to receive them fully, I may require of you the cross."

There is no compromise, no half measure with God's Fatherhood. Little wonder, then, that we try to keep Fatherhood at arm's length, locked away in the attic of our spiritual house.

Yet Jesus Himself spoke of the importance—indeed, the imperative—of knowing the Father. "I must be about My Father's business," He said. And later, "I and the Father are one." And again, "I have come to show you the Father."

Endless, indeed, *is* the fellowship...unlimited *is* the comfort...wondrous *is* the love to which the Son and the Spirit attest—but only when we know the Father aright.

It is into this *knowing* that Jesus came to lead and instruct us.

He seeks to introduce us to a life lived *with* the Father. Not a mere begetting, but a life of ongoing, moment-by-moment intimacy on all levels of humanhood—mind, heart, soul, and will.

> IT IS TOWARD INTIMACY WITH THE FATHER THAT THE SON WOULD GUIDE US.

It is toward intimacy with the Father that the Son would guide us. For such He was born. For such He died.

If we do not take His hand and walk along the upward pathway the Son has marked out for us, following in His footsteps, even those most active among Christian men and women will only be "offspring" of the Father—children *begotten*, but not sons and daughters of *intimacy*.

Let us, therefore, as Thomas Kelly exhorted, "dare to venture together into the inner sanctuary of the soul, where God meets man in awful intimacy."[1]

Do not shrink away from that word, for truly the association He seeks is not "awful." Invert the syllables—full of awe—and discover the key to the great doorway of life, the pathway upward out of the valley!

The fear of the Lord is the beginning of wisdom, says the Proverbs.[2]

What is this fear? The mortal terror of something awful?

A thousand times no!

Rather, it is an openhearted bowing before the *awe-full*—a God *full* of *awe* and mystery and wonder.

Does He truly want to be *my* Father and spend time with *me* and see to *my* every need, *my* every thought? Does He want to take care of *me* and reveal Himself to *me*?

Does He want to fulfill all my *mind* can think to think, all my *heart* feels, all my *soul* invisibly longs for? Does He want to transform my *will* into the most powerful instrument available for the doing of good?

Does He want to give me His business to be about, just like Jesus?

Yes, all this and more awaits us. Of such is life on the mountaintops.

The God of the universe, the Creator of the heavens and the earth, the Father of Jesus Christ Himself desires daily companionship with *me*!

He wants me to call Him *Father*!

ENDNOTES

1. Thomas Kelly, *A Testament of Devotion* (New York: Harper & Row, 1941), p. 55.
2. Prov. 9:10. See also Ps. 111:10 NIV.

5

WHO IS THE FATHER?

CHRISTIANS AND NON-CHRISTIANS, ATHEISTS AND AGNOSTICS, theologians and laymen, thinkers and non-thinkers, pastors and priests, men and women and children alike, possess but hazy and scant images of the sort of being God the Father actually is.

What is His character, His nature? What are His essential purposes in His dealings with man? Who *is* God?

Men and women have been asking variations of this question since time began. Yet because it is so lofty an inquiry, and because the error of the holiness veil-shroud remains so deeply entrenched, they bring a series of devastating misconceptions to it.

Most of us can parrot back phrases and principles we have been taught. Theologians and writers, priests and preachers, lecturers and conference leaders, till and retill the same tired soil of their worn-out doctrines, offering little more than what *they* have been taught. But few really *know* the nature of the One with whom Jesus went out into the hills alone.

Incredibly, we are even afraid to inquire. Somehow we have embraced the notion that God does not want us asking too many questions about Him. The clouds of Sinai still swirl about our heads...and we're a little afraid to look up.

15

GOD: A GOOD FATHER

What mother or father would scold an inquisitive child for the question: "Mommy, Daddy...what are you like? I want to know you more deeply." What joy would fill the heart of the parent hearing such words.

But the keepers of the ecclesiastical doorways tell us *not* to question, *not* to probe, *not* to inquire too extensively into God's character or His eternal purposes. Hungry hearts and active brains threaten their established systems. As long as God is kept distant and unapproachable, the people will look to these valley theologians, like the priests of old, to "interpret" Him for them...rather than climbing up into His lap and gazing into His face for themselves. The fear of stepping outside the orthodoxies of our religious systems has created a new hierarchy of fear just as surely as if we were still held under the thumb of an Old Testament priesthood.

Salvation is not at issue here. A prisoner sitting in a stone cell may receive food every day from a warden he never sees. The food nourishes him and offers him life, though he knows nothing of the hand providing it. And if one day a writ of pardon comes from the hand of a forgiving and gracious judge, the prisoner will be unshackled and full of rejoicing when he walks outside into the air of freedom, though he has never laid eyes on his savior and knows nothing about him.

Likewise, salvation comes through Jesus Christ to millions for whom relationship with the Son seems very near and real and personal...yet who may never meet His Father face-to-face, nor seek to know what manner of Father Jesus repeatedly spoke of.

It is possible—indeed, even likely—to enter into the second birth made available by God's Spirit...yet exist in only a textbook relationship with His Fatherhood.

These Christians are part of God's family, and they have established a certain level of relationship with Son and Spirit. They may evidence genuine spiritual life. With respect to the Father, however, they have a relationship we might describe as "knowing a friend of a friend."

The relationship is one of vague familiarity, not intimacy. Even after years as members of His family, it is possible to know very little about the nature of the Father Jesus so intimately called *Abba*.

We relate to the Father as to the two bookends framing existence. We recognize Him as the vague begetting source of life—the *Alpha*. And we tremble when we think of Him as the severe and terrible judge of sin on the great white throne of eternity—the Omega. Between the two, however, most Catholics and evangelicals, protestants and Jews, live out their lives largely inattentive to that deepest fundamental relationship between child and Father from which they were created to draw every breath. Life between the bookends offers a comfortable and pleasant, social and churchy existence, leaving the larger and all-important purposes of the Father for the next life.

Such is not the kind of life into which Jesus invited His disciples when He said, "Follow Me."[1] It is not the kind of life He lived for—and died for. *Full* fellowship—the "whole measure" of spiritual maturity of which Paul spoke—the "full gospel" Jesus came to reveal, is *fellowship with His Father*.

To move toward intimacy with the Father, therefore, requires that we acknowledge the following with honesty and humble self-examination: It is easier than we may have realized to think we know a great deal "about" God the Father without knowing *Him* personally.

What is the Father like? This is *the* most important question of our existence. It is *the* universal quest.

> *WHAT IS THE FATHER LIKE?* THIS IS *THE* MOST IMPORTANT QUESTION OF OUR EXISTENCE. IT IS *THE* UNIVERSAL QUEST.

Finding the answer and forming a proper heart response to that answer is the ultimate journey upon which our earthly footsteps are bound, the pilgrimage toward our destiny as human beings.

ENDNOTE

1. See Mt. 4:19; Mk. 1:17; Lk. 5:27; Jn. 1:43.

6

THE DIFFICULTY
OF INTIMACY

WHY *IS* FATHERHOOD OBSCURE?

Primarily, of course, because God's holiness and infinitude cannot coexist with the selfish and finite nature of humankind. The Israelites of old could not look upon the face of God lest they die. Moses could not even wear sandals in the presence of God.

There sits a natural and intrinsic gulf between God's perfection and man's humanness—a great distance, a chasm of unlikeness.

That being the case, then, how can we know Him intimately?

Through the Son. God sent the Son that we might see in a man what we could not otherwise behold.

The same chasm doesn't exist between Jesus and ourselves.

He was one of us. He lived, He breathed, He spoke, He ate, He became tired and frustrated, He slept, He experienced relationships, He had both friends and enemies, He had acquaintances who turned against Him. We can read words that actually fell from His lips. His personality and His humanness are graspable.

And Jesus came to tell us: *"The Father is just like Me."*

Even though Jesus said the Father and Son were one, even though He told His disciples, "If you have seen Me, you have seen the Father,"[1] even though He points consistently and *only* to the Father...the Father still remains distant and obscure.

Why?

If we take Jesus at His word, we see that it is the *Father* we are to worship, it is the *Father* whom we are to seek to know, it is the *Father* whose work we are to be about, it is the *Father* with whom we are to walk in close and daily friendship...as Jesus Himself did.

> IF WE TAKE JESUS AT HIS WORD, WE SEE THAT IT IS THE *FATHER* WE ARE TO WORSHIP, IT IS THE *FATHER* WHOM WE ARE TO SEEK TO KNOW.

Thus exists the great dichotomy: God the Father is holy and infinite, we are sinful and finite. We are separate from Him. He is invisible to human eyes. He does not speak with audible words. No man since the Garden but Moses has seen His face. Though His invisible fingerprints are everywhere, His footprints mark no *place* upon the earth. In all finite human ways of "knowing," God the Father is unknowable. *Yet only in knowing Him do we live as He purposed us to live.*

Therein lies the mystery of God's Fatherhood.

Words we all are familiar with and have heard from the days of our spiritual infancy will immediately spring to mind in explanation of this phenomenon that lies at the core of the Christian message. Words such as, "Jesus bridged the gap"... "Through the cross we come back into fellowship with God"... "Christ atoned for our sins"... "Jesus reconciles us to God"... "Jesus Christ is our mediator making peace between God and sinful man."

True enough every one—and thank God for making provision in the midst of a dilemma of eternal proportions from which we could never have extricated ourselves.

These explain the underpinning foundation of the Christian faith. They clarify why salvation is possible, and why those appropriating their truths no longer walk under the inevitable doom of sin.

Again we rejoice and say, *thank God* for these truths!

But alas, such explanations are chiefly theological. For most—I do not say all—who call themselves Christians, and certainly for all who do not, they accomplish little to practically lead into that moment-by-moment, walking-and-talking, child-with-Father intimacy that Jesus enjoyed with His Father. We stop short of the very thing Jesus said was His deepest heart's desire—that we know His Father as He did.

ENDNOTE

1. See Jn. 14:8.

7

LOOKING UPWARD

LAUNCHING OUT FROM SECURE DOCTRINAL HOMES one has known for years can be more than a little fearful. The first steps are often timid ones.

Though fear of the Lord is the beginning of wisdom, we're often so fogged in the traditions of men that we don't inquire beyond them to find out what the Lord's wisdom actually might be. We're especially dubious of any so-called *new* doctrine that seeks to explain things in ways we're unaccustomed to. We're afraid because we've been taught to be afraid.

Truly I understand, dear friends. I myself lived in the valley for many years. How well I recall my own first tentative steps beyond what I had been taught. How afraid I was that I might overstep the traditional bounds of my spiritual training in leaving the comfort of the low-lying terrain I knew so well.

How reassuring it was in time to realize that the footsteps I was following out of the valley were the Master's own.

Jesus sought His Father alone in the hills...and He invites us to accompany Him upward.

If you cannot altogether leave your timidity, at least do not let it detain you. In time you will look back and realize that your fears have vanished in the fresh lofty air of the mountains where God lives.

Quiet yourself just now.

Put away pen that would underline, take notes, or scribble thoughts in the margin. Rather, let your thoughts rest for a few moments, and let your heart speak.

We have arrived at the edge of the valley. The first step along the upward path awaits us. We begin now to move toward a new realm of getting to know our Father.

Pray with me, will you.

Father of Jesus, God of the universe, perhaps I have not known You as intimately as You would like to know me. It matters not the cause. This moment has come in my life when I have become aware that I want to know You with the kind of intimacy with which Your Son Jesus knew You. I want to walk and fellowship and interact with You in a close and daily way. I want to know You fully, or at least as fully as is possible. But with the recognition that I don't know You as well as I might comes also the realization that I don't know how to get to know You.

So I ask You to help me. I want to know You, and to do so I need Your guidance. I open my mind and my heart and my soul to You. I ask You to begin turning them in new directions—toward all that Your Fatherhood would speak into the depths of my being. Begin strengthening my will, too, so that it becomes trained in pointing the way You would have me go. Help me to think, to feel, and to choose in harmony with Your Fatherhood in my life.

Reveal Yourself to me. Show me what You are like, show me Your nature and Your character. Open me to all You would make known to me about Yourself.

Now, please set down this book, close your eyes, and pray this prayer again. Do not repeat the words written on these pages, but pray quietly in your own words, giving to the Father the open and humble expressions of your own heart.

This is a prayer any man, woman, or child can pray, whatever their level of spiritual development.

To all who open themselves, and humbly ask for the Father to make Himself known, worlds of *true knowing* will slowly and gently begin to open...not because of any how-to lists, but from being in the presence of the Father.

By continuing to pray your own version of this prayer daily, bringing it into our progress together and to the Scriptures you read, you will find yourself gradually perceiving truths on newer and deeper levels, at the most unexpected times and places. This will be the Father speaking to you. He always answers prayer. If you spoke the words in earnest to Him, you can be sure He will give answers into your heart and mind.

Not all at once. In fact, no change may be apparent for hours, days, maybe even years. But as the desires of your prayers are infused more deeply into your being, the Father will answer them. Such prayers will open doors and windows into the higher realms of the Father's being and purposes.

> *REVEAL TRUTH TO ME. SHOW ME HOW TO CALL YOU FATHER. DRAW ME INTO YOUR PRESENCE.*

With every new step we take on this journey, silently lift up to God the heart-opening reaffirmation: *Reveal truth to me. Show me how to call You Father. Draw me into Your presence.*

Do you seek practicalities?

You have just prayed the most vital and practical prayer in all the universe—the prayer that God longs to hear His creatures pray.

With those sixteen simple words, you have begun a quest that will change the course of your spiritual life! As long as you continue to orient your inner self Father-ward, it is a quest that will continue to lead you to new heights, which will, in turn, open into realms of new depths of "knowing" throughout this life...and throughout all eternity.

We are on a journey to discover the One whom it delighted Jesus' heart to seek. This journey, upon which the Son invites us, is a quest of discovery.

He bids us rise with Him early, a long while before day, while the world yet sleeps. He invites us to accompany Him into the quiet hills alone. As our Guide and Friend, He bids us toward the mountains, there to discover intimacy with His Father...and ours.

8

GETTING TO KNOW

WHAT IS *KNOWING*?

Two ways of knowing exist, do they not? We say that we "know" things, and we say that we "know" people.

The former refers to *information* one possesses. You say you know facts and data concerning the multiplication table, the discovery of America, or the content of the Book of Ephesians. This is knowledge of an intellectual sort, most of which you have been taught. There need be no particular emotional connection with such knowing. It merely exists as raw data in your brain.

People, on the other hand, are known not through brain cells, but by an emotive connection that draws them into fellowship. Bonds, shared interests, common goals, similar outlooks, mutual admiration, time spent together interacting on many levels about many things—these and a hundred other subtleties draw individuals together into the kind of relationship that eventually results in the phrase, "I *know* you…and I recognize that you *know* me."

The first kind of knowing is learned. It can, though doesn't always, come instantaneously. It is often, though not always, taught.

The other comes through interaction. It *never* comes instantaneously. It *cannot* be taught.

I can't know you by reading a book about you. I know you by getting to know *you*.

27

This unfortunate use of the same word for two very distinctive phenomena leads to a great deal of confusion in our attempt to "know" God.

We read, we study, we are taught, we probe the Scriptures, we discuss, we listen to the declarations of pastors, preachers, priests, teachers, and authors, gaining a great wealth of useful and perhaps very true and often biblically correct information. What we assemble in the process, however, is a mere informational matrix of knowledge of the first sort. It is something like putting together a mathematical chart, into whose boxes we gather what data we can learn about God. When enough of the chart is filled in, we begin to conclude that we *know* God. In reality we have only *learned* Him.

If I want to know *you*, I cannot do so by compiling a data spreadsheet of your characteristics. I can't *learn* you...I must "get to know" you.

It's an altogether different kind of knowing. I must spend time with you, I must cultivate bonds of relationship with you.

The Germans, precise and ordered people that they are, have three different words to distinguish the different ways of "knowing."

Wissen indicates the knowing of information, being informed about a certain matter. It denotes the possession of factual knowledge.

Kennen, on the other hand, is to know a person.

Kennenlernen—literally, "to learn to know"—describes the intermediary act of *getting to know* an individual. This compound word reveals the interconnection between the two ways of knowing, pointing out the essential, qualitative *process* involved.

The question before each one of us, therefore, becomes: Into which category does our "knowledge" of God the Father fall—the *informational* or the *intimate*?

Which brings us to another important question: What manner of "knowing" do you seek?

No judgment will be passed upon those seeking informative, factual knowledge. Such is a useful and necessary component of life. And informative, factual information about God is a helpful component of spiritual growth.

However, since such will not be the focus here, those desirous of accumulating data with which to fill in the charts and tables of their *Wissen* regarding God's Fatherhood will no doubt find this a most unpractical journey. We are taking no notebooks with us, only stout climbing shoes.

There will be little to write down as we progress, no lists and steps toward increased spirituality, no keys to self-analysis and fulfillment, few gems to jot in the margins of your reference Bibles. You may listen to my every word, and yet conclude, "There is nothing here, only vague unpracticalities."

> WE MUST MOVE UPWARD INTO HIS PRESENCE.

Kennen—not *Wissen*—is the object of our pursuit, through the process of *Kennenlernen*.

Kennenlernen does not come through lists, nor through what the modernity of the valley world deems "practicalities," nor through anecdotal or shallow humorous examples of this truth or that. No informational matrix, no cognitive analysis, no cerebral dissection of this book or even the Scriptures can open the door that will enable one to "get to know" the Father.

To do that, we must move upward into His presence.

9

SECRETS ABOUT OUR MAKER

BEGINNING OUR JOURNEY WITH A PRAYER, asking God to reveal truth to us, is the only appropriate starting point. Indeed, by no other means than the Father's revelation can truth come. Nothing merely *said* here will open truth to your inner ears.

As you prayed in Chapter 7, tiptoeing gingerly into that silent chamber within your heart where dwells the Spirit of God, did everything previously abstract about His Fatherhood suddenly become clarified in your mind?

Of course not.

Kennenlernen takes time.

There are few prayers God is more anxious to answer than that one. But He is in no hurry. His purposes cannot be rushed. He *will* answer your heart's desire, but quietly and in His own chosen manner and time.

Nor will revelation come primarily in the region of your brain. He will reveal Himself into your heart when, and in quietly subtle ways, you least expect.

How do we then begin to enter into those still, quiet regions where revelation comes?

By training ourselves to look *inside*, into the heart of those things God has made. There is the first place the Fatherhood of God begins to come into focus, for we begin to "get to know" Him by looking for His character and personality within His world.

God created the universe full of secrets, mysteries, and dichotomies.

Without exaggeration, we can say that in all things there are multiple levels at which they can be seen and understood.

Everything!

In the physical creation, in scriptural truths, in the animal kingdom, in human relationships...everywhere there are *surface* appearances that contain *subsurface* meanings, implications, and significance.

> THE WORLD'S MYSTERIES ARE OUR INITIAL FATHERHOOD SCHOOL.

Learning to look into those hidden, secret meanings gives us the eyesight necessary to begin beholding our Father. The world's mysteries are our initial Fatherhood school.

With the eyes one may cast his gaze upon a tree and perceive a trunk enclosed with hard bark, to all appearances stiff and dead and lifeless. But deep inside, the secret of life itself flows up and down unseen by any eye but God's. Ah, the mysteries contained within that wood!

Deep below, in the earth, where all is dark and wet, roots draw nourishment from the soil, through an osmosis no one completely understands, and pull those needful nutrients from out of the ground, through the flow of sap, up through the majestic trunk, out the branches, where at length are produced leaves, buds, and tender shoots of new growth. The leaves in turn point their green faces to the sun, and drink from its rays to bring life into the tree from the sky, mirroring above the ground the activity of the roots below.

The sun communicates with the black interior of the earth, the clouds send rain from the sky to moisten the soil—all these wonders of nature function in marvelous unity of purpose and life. What no thousand geniuses together could create in a laboratory—the miracle of life—flourishes in grand profusion all around us every instant, from each blade of grass the foot steps on, to the mightiest oak or redwood.

What a silent nature-symphony of miracles at work in perfect, invisible harmony! It is possible, however, never to behold a hint of all this.

Many never do.

For the mysteries of life are *hidden.*

One can walk through a forest without apprehending the music of nature in process beneath the bark that surrounds the trunks, underfoot inside the ground, in the leaves waving in the breeze.

The mysteries exist, none would question that. The question is—who sees them? Who hears the music of the universe?

It is fearfully easy *not* to see the mysteries nor hear the music. It is possible to wander through one's day oblivious to the hidden secrets of life so close they touch us on every level.

When one holds a bright, perfect, fragrant rose in his hand, well opened and lush, who cannot marvel at the spectacular display of God's creative hand?

Why do we admire the rose? Is it for the wondrous colors and pleasant aroma? Are these bright petals what we would call the glory of the rosebush?

Of course.

But the rose has deeper truths and secrets to reveal...*if* we have the kind of eyes Jesus told us to develop—the kind of eyes that see below and into and *inside.*

Truths about the One who made it!

The true glories of the rose speak their deepest messages at a far more profound level...their mysteries...their secrets...the glimpses they give us of eternal things....the glimpses they give us of the Father.

Have you held dry kernels of grain in your hand...of wheat, rye, or corn? Does not a reverence well up inside as you rub them between your fingers...the truth dawning that the very mystery of life itself exists within those tiny grains?

Where is the life of an egg? In the yolk.

What do the rose, the kernel, and the egg all have in common?

They all contain life. *Hidden* life...deep inside in the center...where the physical eye cannot see.

Life that is invisible except to those eyes that search for it—and therein lies the mystery!

10

A Few Minutes With the Father

Can you imagine the Father beside you, accompanying you in this pilgrimage of learning to see Him and His world differently?

For most of us, such an exercise will be extremely difficult. Somehow we can visualize Jesus. But personalizing the Father puts a far greater strain on our spiritual imaginations.

And yet I hope a familiarity is beginning to set in that will enable you to do so. Your friendship with Him has begun.

As you progress, therefore, imagine the Father smiling beside you. It is He who has beckoned you upward and mountainward, not me. For whatever reason you are reading these words at this moment—whether you bought the book you now hold, or were lent it by a friend, or found it in a library or it caught your eye on someone's coffee table—the Father Himself drew you to it, not the title or the look of the cover or my name.

> The Father drew you to read these words. And now He is gradually making Himself more and more real.

The Father wanted to make Himself known to you. He drew you to read these words. And now He is gradually making Himself more and more real.

And as astonishing as it may be at first, when we look into His face we find a smile, not the theologians' scowl.

The Father is *smiling*…at you and me!

"I have something to show you," He says. "A small truth, but a worthwhile one. If you can understand, it will be the first of many such truths I will show you."

You glance toward Him, and return His smile. What might you say?

"Oh, yes, Father!" would we not reply with all our heart. "I am eager for whatever You have to show me. Please show me more of what Your Fatherhood means."

"Do you find the upward course pleasant, now that the mists are thinning?"

"Yes."

"Then let us look more to what this high country has to tell us."

A brief pause follows, then He asks an unexpected question.

"Kneel down," He says, releasing the hand by which He has been leading you. "Scoop up a handful of the earth around one of these roses…now look at what you have picked up," He says. "Is there anything special about it?"

"It is only dirt," you say.

"Do you see color there, do you smell the perfume of the rose?"

You shake your head.

But in truth, in God's idea of what makes a rose a rose, all those qualities are there in your hand.

Perhaps the glory of the rose is indeed embodied in the flower you lift to your nostrils. But the life, the mystery—they are contained in the handful of soil you scooped up from below.

Once you clip a stalk from the plant, immediately the blossom begins to die. Yet as long as its roots extend deep into the earth, the plant lives and thrives and continues to bear a most wonderful profusion of color. But take it out of the soil, and instantly the life is gone.

Curious, is it not, that this low, despised commodity we call dirt should be the transmitter of life itself to everything that grows on the face of God's earth? God hides life in the most out-of-the-way, hidden places.

Now glance up into the treetops around you, then to the sky beyond.

Can you sense the beginnings of a change already? Do you feel more in touch with the high-reaching instinct of your nature?

Breathe in deeply. Does it not seem good to know that the Father is nearby, that you can come and go in His presence without anxiety, and that He has many pleasant secrets to reveal to you?

Most of all it is wonderful to realize that there is a smile on His face, and that He welcomes you into His presence.

Every moment spent thus with the Father, listening to Him and conversing with Him, deepens the knowing, and adds meaning when we look up and call Him Father.

11

THE GREATEST
HIDDEN MYSTERY OF ALL

AGAIN IT IS TIME FOR THE REMINDER: BE IN NO HURRY IN YOUR QUEST.
It will take time to develop the intimacy you prayerfully seek.

Close your eyes. Descend inwardly to your quiet closet of communion,
and there whisper again: "Reveal truth to me. Show me how to call You
Father. Draw me into Your presence."

Then throughout the days that follow, as you begin practicing more and
more frequently this exercise of conscious inner retreat to your quiet center,
cultivating the habit of living simultaneously in the sanctuary you share
only with Him and at the same time going on about the duties of your life,
you will gradually discover your inner eyes growing more keen.

Practice observing the fingerprint of the Father about you. It is the first
lesson of the low hills, and that by which the mountains above become
increasingly visible.

All living things have much to tell us of their Maker...truths hidden
from all but the most diligent and seeking of eyes.

Why is it so?

One would think God would desire that everyone know all they can
about Him. To our reasoning, it would seem His object would be to make all

truth, and especially that which specifically concerns His being and character, clear and plain and visible.

Why, then, are there so many mysteries?

Why is so much about God hard to understand? Why is truth, of all life's commodities, the most difficult to come by? Why are the deepest things the most obscure?

Among the most significant words Jesus spoke, and among those most vital to be heeded, are those He repeated often, "He who has ears to hear, let him hear."[1]

To feel the full weight of this powerful command with which Jesus punctuated His important teachings, one must realize that He was not merely talking to Pharisees. He was also speaking to His followers.

Jesus knew well the divining truth that divides all the universe—that it is possible to see, and yet *not* see.

When speaking of our need to discover truths God has hidden away, we cannot limit the discussion to matters of belief and nonbelief. For Christians too—perhaps above all—are required to discover deep truths *within* the walk of faith...truths that often aren't part of daily life. The capacity to see with inner eyesight is not developed nor emphasized in our contemporary assemblies as an intrinsic aspect of spiritual growth.

It is a matter of learning to *see*...with the right eyes. And in a very real sense, it represents the beginning of spiritual maturity.

God's ways are often curious, and full of mystery. Why is it that He seems to *hide* Himself, enclosing life and truth within mysterious outer shells that seem different than what they contain?

Yet whether we know *why* He chose it, this is one of God's methods. And somehow, too, another principle can also be recognized: Throughout every aspect of His work, God reveals truth only to those who seek it.

What a paradox we are given in Romans 1:19-20: Man can know all about God's nature by the things He has made, yet the Lord says truth has been obscured so that men will see and *not* understand. And the greater the truth, the more obscure He makes it, so that the finding of it must be all the greater a quest.

A huge screening process operates in constant interplay with world events and circumstances and teachings and relationships—a process screening out truth seekers from self-seekers, just as farmers separate wheat from chaff at harvest time.

Truth seekers discover layer upon layer of truth as they progress through life, whereas *self-seekers* become increasingly blind to truth by the thickening screen of their self-preoccupation.

Therefore, God encloses the deepest truths in husks, so that truth seekers, those rare individuals who want to know His ways, whatever the cost, will dig and search and pray and seek...until light dawns in their hearts.

God chose to "hide His face" from the eyes of man, and to reveal His being and character through the things He has made. He sent the Savior of men, the one who would be King over all the earth, the very King of kings, in a form none would recognize—a baby born of common folk.

George MacDonald wrote:

> They all were looking for a king
>> To slay their foes, and lift them high:
> Thou cam'st a little baby thing
>> That made a woman cry.

Why this is the process, who can know? But it *is* the process, inverted as it may be from human equations of reason.

To *see* as Jesus commanded requires looking past the husks and shells, deep into the heart of all things. It requires spending more and more time in our own quiet centers where inner vision is cultivated.

If it is true that God surrounds the largest of His truths in the thickest of husks, we would expect the greatest of His secrets to be among the most difficult to find. And indeed, the deepest secret of His character is His *Fatherhood*, lying at the very core of the Godhead.

God has allowed the Sonship of His nature to be "seeable" to the eyes of man through Jesus. But God's Fatherhood is hidden from earthbound eyes. It must be penetrated in an altogether different manner.

The greatest truth to be found, therefore, is the answer to this question: *Who is God the Father, and what is He like?*

> GOD'S FATHERHOOD IS HIDDEN FROM EARTHBOUND EYES. IT MUST BE PENETRATED IN AN ALTOGETHER DIFFERENT MANNER.

O God, help us understand. Reveal Your truth to us, we ask You with all earnestness and humility.

Our Father, increase our hunger to know You and to discover Your ways! Give us minds and hearts and hands courageous to climb high, even unto weariness! Let us faint not. Bring Your dawn to our hearts!

ENDNOTE

1. See Mk. 4:9; Lk. 8:8; Lk. 14:35 NIV.

12

GOD'S FATHERHOOD

ARE SOME OF YOU GROWING IMPATIENT WITH ALL THIS TALK of mysteries and hidden truths, saying to yourselves, "Get on with it...tell us about Fatherhood"?

I'm sorry, but I cannot *tell* you about Fatherhood. I can only help you discover it for yourself. And the first important part of that process is disciplining yourself to *see* in new ways. This is where it all begins. It is a slow, quiet learning process that cannot be hastened.

Why have we been talking about eggs and trees and roses and grains? Because we have to train our eyes to *apprehend* Fatherhood in unexpected places. Nothing I can say to you will be of the least benefit without such apprehending eyes.

Fatherhood exists...all about us. We have to learn to *see* it... first in grains of wheat and in the bud of the rose.

When these lessons are learned, the Spirit will take us to higher plateaus, until at last we are capable of dwelling among the very peaks themselves. To get there, however, we must learn to *discern* the Father's fingerprints in the world about us.

This is the first step in *knowing*. When we see His fingerprint, then we can begin to discover what kind of Father caused that fingerprint. Thus, slowly by degrees, His character begins to dawn in our heart.

The most important truth in all the universe can be stated in four words: *God is our Father.*

The world literally hangs together by this central truth. Without divine Fatherhood, there is no life, there is no love...there is no universe.

To the extent we apprehend God's Fatherhood will our life be integrated, whole, and complete in relationship to the Creator who made us and to the surroundings in which He has placed us.

THE MOST IMPORTANT TRUTH IN ALL THE UNIVERSE CAN BE STATED IN FOUR WORDS: *GOD IS OUR FATHER*

Seeking and finding God's Fatherhood is *the* great story, the essence of history, the meaning of the hidden thread weaving through every human life. It is the story of God's people in the Bible. It is the reason Jesus came. It is the very essence of Jesus' two mighty prayers on the night before His death—with His disciples, and later in the garden as they slept.

In this pilgrimage we have undertaken, we are following in the footsteps of our Lord, who throughout His life, had to seek God and pray for increasing depths to be revealed to Him concerning the divine Fatherhood.

Imagine it—even Jesus Himself had to seek this "knowing" of His Father's character and being, in just the same way we do! He was occasionally in doubt about His Father's will. He had to "get to know" the Father too.

Indeed, He is our Brother...our example and our trailblazer in this quest!

When we read the Gospels with our newly trained eyes, we begin to see that God's Fatherhood is the single truth toward which Jesus *always* points. It was the entire focal point of His mission on earth.

In this mission, however, Jesus forged new ground. Aside from a few instances, throughout the Old Testament God had not been perceived as a Father. There was no doctrine of the Trinity—no concept of Father, no knowledge of Son, no awareness of Holy Spirit. Yahweh was "one." *Father* was arguably the last term anyone would have used to describe Him.

Nor was the Jews' religion in Jesus' day a personal one. They viewed God primarily as Lawgiver and Judge. Moses and David walked in intimate friendship with God, but not so the masses. The Law was to be obeyed, and the Almighty Judge called Yahweh stood ready to render judgment when it was broken.

Greek and Roman secularists and philosophers, on the other hand, viewed "God" or "the gods" either as an abstract principle (in the way that Caesar was "god") or pure myth.

Nowhere in the theological or philosophical world of Jesus' time, then, was divine character equated with Fatherhood.

Jesus did not merely "make all things new" by bringing the new life of the second birth. He made new as well the prevailing perception of who God was. He broke apart the "oneness" of God's being into its three constituent parts.

He declared, "I am the *Son*. I will make life possible by My example, My teaching, and by giving My life for you. When I go from you I will send the *Spirit* to reveal truth and give you power to live the new life."

And throughout his life, over and over Jesus emphasized: "Come to My *Father*, pray to My *Father*, know My *Father*, seek My *Father*. I will show you the way to Him…but *He* is the source of life itself."

Fatherhood was the reason Jesus could work miracles, the reason He was born into a family, the reason He died, the reason He rose. The Atonement and the Resurrection were the Father's doing, wrought and made possible through Jesus' obedience. Jesus had nothing else in all the world to do—and He said so—but to point us to the Father.

"If you have seen Me," He said, "you have seen the Father."[1]

Thus, the question arises: Have we truly seen either Jesus *or* the Father? Seen them as He meant us to see them?

This is why we must train our eyes to see, first in the small things, that we might then behold the larger.

It behooves us to look with more dedication and diligence into the Gospels to discover the true nature of both Father and Son. For learning to live as the Father's children is the only means whereby the world will come to know the Father whom Jesus came to reveal.

ENDNOTE

1. See Jn. 14:8 NIV.

13

ABBA, FATHER

REALITIES OF SPIRITUAL TRUTH CAN BE SEEN WITH EITHER the eyes of the flesh or the eyes of the spirit. When *spiritual* truth is viewed with the eyes of the *flesh*, it is seen as through a glass darkly, and complete truth is incapable of being seen.

Therefore, it is not only unbelievers who misunderstand the ways of God, but also Christians, and especially theologians who have set themselves more to explain God than *know* Him as their Father. These experts in God's holiness who say He cannot look upon man in his sinful state would do well to find out what Jesus called Him.

It is possible to scrutinize every New Testament doctrine imaginable and to fill in with a certain accuracy an intellectually consistent informational grid about God and His work…yet all the while to be able to make out but an incomplete, sketchy, and truncated version of spiritual reality.

When dogma-loving rationality leads the way, building precept upon precept from earlier doctrines put forth by human intellects, looking only to the surface of scriptural truth, a curtailed theology results, satisfying the contorted equations set by human reason but not unearthing the deepest mysteries of God's nature hidden in Scripture.

Between the clearly discernible regions of truth and falsehood lies a gray shadowy land of partial truth, whose inhabitants live according to spiritual principles, but apprehend them with *fleshly* eyes. The reality of God's

Fatherhood, however, cannot be discovered there, but only in a region of true spiritual seeing. The equations of God's character and purpose cannot be solved by human theologians who keep Him at arm's length.

Those who still dwell in these gray shadows, though they have devoted a lifetime to studying the New Testament through the austere eyes of their French mentor, remarkably have not yet fully accepted the truth that everything changed when Jesus came.

Salvation became personal. Living as God's sons and daughters became personal. God's being became personal.

Though some perceive the triune personality of the Godhead in the opening chapters of Genesis, God did not make the constituent parts of His nature discernible to man until the fullness of time when Jesus came to earth.

At that point He peeled away the shell, the husk. He tore down the veil that had hidden His presence. He opened up the "oneness" of Yahweh that had existed at the core of Judaism throughout the Old Testament and said to man, "Here are several distinctive parts of My nature. Now I want you to relate yourselves personally and individually with all three."

For the first time He allowed man to look inside, into the very depths of His being. Not just *peer* inside for a momentary glimpse... *He invited us to come live with Him there!*

What was it men and women found when they looked beyond the veil, when they probed the depths of God's being?

They discovered the Son, Jesus Himself! A sinless Man, a loving Friend, an understanding Brother who was willing to die for them, that they might not perish from sin.

When He went away, they further discovered a consoling, guiding, truth-loving Spirit, the very Spirit of God whom Jesus had promised He would send to remain with them forever.

But what else did they discover?

Just what Jesus told them they would find—a loving, tender, forgiving, patient, warm, generous Father who wants only the best for His children, and will spare nothing that He can do to lavish His love upon them. It is a picture of God's being and purpose in human life far different from what those of Jesus' day imagined.

The writer of Hebrews opened his letter with the magnificent words that illuminate this huge shift in divine revelation: "In the past God spoke to our forefathers through the prophets at many times and in various ways, but in these last days He has spoken to us by His Son."

The Sonship of Jesus necessitated a divine Fatherhood, a way of seeing God that was utterly foreign to the prevailing religious mentality of Jesus' day. Alas, all these centuries later, we have still not apprehended what the Son was trying to tell us about the Father He loved so dearly!

> THE SONSHIP OF JESUS NECESSITATED A DIVINE FATHERHOOD, A WAY OF SEEING GOD THAT WAS UTTERLY FOREIGN TO THE PREVAILING RELIGIOUS MENTALITY OF JESUS' DAY.

Of all the changes brought by Jesus in what constituted a "spiritual life," intimacy with God as Father was the most astonishing and revolutionary.

Jesus rose before daybreak and went out in the hills to be alone with God. Who was it He sought there?

The Incomprehensible Almighty Sovereign King of the universe? That Great and Dreadful Holy Presence upon whose face no man could look and live? The Omnipotent Lawgiver of Old Testament Judaism? The Holy One who could not abide sin in His Presence? The Judge of the universe who would decide the ultimate eternal fate of every creature?

No.

Jesus rose before daybreak to be alone with His Father, to speak intimately with Him, calling him *Abba*.

Abba was the term a child used when he addressed his father. It was probably the word Jesus used when talking to Joseph...Abba...father... *daddy*. It conveyed warmth and family respect, but in regard to God it was an unheard-of familiarity.

Within Judaism there is no indication it had ever been a form of address toward God. Jesus was the first so to employ the word.

If Jesus was truly God's Son, then it is understandable that He would make use of this form of intimate address. But the thunderous truth is this: *He told all men to follow His example.*

When Jesus told His disciples how to speak to God, He gave them the right to speak with intimacy and familiarity. The Lord's prayer did not begin, "Almighty divine Sovereign..." It began, *Our Father*—the intimacy of divine *Daddy*ness with the Creator of the heavens and earth!

In that moment, the entire spiritual foundation of our relationship with God was changed: Jesus declared that God was forevermore to be our *daddy*!

You may approach the Father closely and personally now, He said— yourselves!

The God of fire and thunder, the God upon whom no man can look, the Holy and Almighty, the Sovereign of Sinai, the great and terrible has now also become your *Daddy...Abba.*

He loves you and will now forgive you your sin. You have only to go to Him.

The veil that hid the Holy of Holies is rent in two. We are invited into His presence, there to dwell with Him in continual intimacy.

14

IMAGING THE WORLD'S MOST LOVING DADDY

IMAGINE YOURSELF FOR A MOMENT, AS WE WALK ALONG IN OUR QUEST after the high places of faith, an orphan. What would it be like never to have known an earthly father? What an emptiness in life that would be, one that some individuals know all too well.

Imagine what Jesus might say to you in introducing you to *His* Father.

"Come, My brother, My sister," He says. "I want you to meet My Daddy. He is the most wonderful Father imaginable. I have told Him about you. He wants to adopt you as His very own child. He desires that you become part of our family."

You can hardly believe what you have just heard!

What could be more wonderful—to have a father who wants you to be his very *own*! Never had you dreamed such good fortune would come to you!

Eagerly you take the hand of Jesus and follow Him as He leads you. On the way you daydream about what this "most wonderful Father" could be like.

Jesus called Him wonderful, so that must mean He is full of love. How could He be anything but kind and generous and patient, attentive and interested in your thoughts, forgiving of your mistakes and shortcomings?

If He is anything like Jesus, He must be all those things. Jesus said He was like His Father, and you have known Jesus long enough to know what a kind and loving friend He is.

Surely this wonderful Father must take care of His children, protecting them from harm, providing for their needs, comforting them in distress.

He must be warm and tender and compassionate, the kind of Father upon whose lap no child would hesitate to climb, there to snuggle against His bosom within the wrap of his large and kindhearted arms.

He must be a smiling Father, who lavishes His young one with kisses and hugs as He whispers, "I love you, My child. You are dear and precious to Me. I will keep My arms around you forever and as long as you will let Me. You may choose to get down, but I will never push you off My lap, nor send you away. It is My delight to love you, and to know that you love Me."

He might be stern, you think to yourself. Surely a perfect Father would not put up with misbehavior. He might even have to discipline you from time to time. But you would not mind that so much because you know He would do so because He loves you, and wants you to grow better.

But some of you, my readers, may find it unfortunate that the term *father* occupies such a pivotal role in God's nature. In many minds, the word conjures up images contradictory to these pleasant daydreams.

Rather than what we have just imagined, today's father is often the butt of sitcom jokes and has a hard time getting his own children to obey. He is either a watered-down nonentity or the scapegoat for the rest of his family's problems and personality hang-ups.

In the ancient patriarchal societies to which Jesus spoke, however, the father was the vital and central figure. A Roman father had power of life or death over his children. A good father could be extraordinarily good, a bad father could be extraordinarily bad.

Western culture is no longer patriarchal. Therefore, when we say "father," we are not thinking of the same image Jesus was. Surely, modernism says, there must be a more appropriate word and image we could use. Indeed, to meet this "need" and to be certain to offend no feminist ears, some new translations have emasculated the divine *He* altogether, replacing it with the more suitable "Personness" of God.

Father, however, was the term Jesus used. God was not His mother, not His divine "person," but His *Father*.

To escape the asphyxiating fogs of valley misperceptions, our thinking must widen—not to throw away the earthly forms of the word, but rather to cast aside the shackles and constraints they impose upon our capacity to see God as He truly is.

HOW MUCH LARGER MIGHT TRUE AND PERFECT FATHERHOOD BE?

How much larger might true and perfect Fatherhood be?

As we thus widen our image of Fatherhood beyond its earthly constraints, a startling truth results: The masculine *and* feminine forms of earthly in-God's-image-ness become drawn up into a unifying whole. Human motherhood and fatherhood *both* combine to make up this divine picture.

Women who take offense at the masculinity said to be inherent in God's Fatherhood may now find themselves joined by men taking offense at femininity entering the divine personality.

Make no mistake. This joint masculinity and femininity cannot be fully envisioned according to any earthly images of either. Within the Godhead they are taken to higher levels, glorified, fulfilled, given their perfect expression as God intended all the creation to reflect distinctive aspects of His nature.

We are being given a place to live within the divine "familyness" of the very Godhead!

Why do we begin thus, with the *imagination*? Are we not bound to come to know God the Father on the basis of what Scripture tells us?

Certainly.

The imagination is merely a doorway.

God has placed the instinct toward Fatherhood deep within every human breast. Everything in us, by nature, points toward our Father, including the imagination. When one attempts to imagine God, therefore, free from preconceptions to the contrary, the compass of God-created instinct cannot help but point in a generally true direction.

These are not fruitless and vain imaginings, but rather the God-implanted instinct after true Fatherhood expressing itself through the imagination. I happen to believe one of the reasons He created imagination in the first place was for this very purpose.

The imagination *wants* to bring good and kind and loving images to mind. God put those visions of Himself within us, so that we would know what His Fatherhood is like.

15

A Thick Husk

Why is it difficult to imagine pure and unreserved goodness at the intrinsic core of Fatherhood?

Because the husks are so thick surrounding the earthly images with which we are familiar. The imagination is not an aspect of the human disposition we have allowed to further spiritual growth. In fact, it is customary to consider it as emerging out of man's fallen nature.

Not so. Imagination, like everything God created, is good.

One who cannot imagine the Father and conceive of what He is like will have difficulty scaling the peaks still ahead. An unimaginative outlook will make of faith a monotonous affair, forever enfeebling the capacity to walk fully with Him.

Henceforth we will make more and more use of the imagination as a God-given tool, a walking stick to help us in our climb to the spiritual high places, stretching our capacity to dwell in Fatherhood with Him. Jesus told stories to create images in the mind, in the imagination, then used those images to explain spiritual principles.

As we have seen, every atom of the universe reflects something about its Creator's being and personality and nature. The divine fingerprint exists everywhere.

In the very act of creation, God left His mark. In all He has ever touched, His fingerprint remains. No erasing agent exists with the capacity to rub out the identifying signature. To know God requires learning to behold those invisible fingerprint lines. We must then use our new ways of seeing and our imagination to identify His signature and to apprehend His Fatherhood in those fingerprints.

Why did God institute earthly fatherhood?

Was it only so men and women could bring forth sons and daughters to keep the human race alive? As we inquired earlier of God, is the reason earthly fathers exist chiefly one of begetting...or is there a greater purpose?

Yes, certainly...but what?

He created earthly fathers primarily to offer a picture of what *He* is like.

Fathers, however, don't do a very good job of showing us God's nature.

The mystery deepens.

God created roses, and they perfectly fulfill their calling. God created the sun, the sky, and the heavens to reflect His glory, and they too fulfill their callings. God created the animal kingdom, and every animal, large and small, fulfills its inborn calling.

God created earthly fatherhood to reflect His nature more than all these others...yet earthly fathers do *not* fulfill this most holy calling.

The physical husk surrounding the spiritual truth is indeed a thick one. How are we to penetrate it?

Why did God select the imperfect to reflect the perfect?

Remember, the greater the truth, the more obscure God makes it, so that the finding of it must require all the greater a quest.

> THE GREATER THE TRUTH, THE MORE OBSCURE GOD MAKES IT, SO THAT THE FINDING OF IT MUST REQUIRE ALL THE GREATER A QUEST.

The process of discovering God's Fatherhood is multidirectional and multidimensional. It isn't a matter of writing down attributes and adopting prescriptions that say, "God is such-and-such," and then saying to oneself, "Ah, now I grasp God's Fatherhood."

God's Fatherhood, the *one* truth He wants all men and women to discover, is—because it is the *largest* truth—one of the most obscured to worldly vision.

Ah, God our Father, do we doubt Your wisdom? Give us eyes to see that we might behold Your purposes in the midst of our earthbound reasonings. Open our eyes wide, Father, to the worlds of Fatherhood You would illuminate within us!

16

IMPERFECT VESSELS

IN FATHERHOOD ITSELF, THOUGH WE DON'T READILY SEE IT, God has left the divine impression of His being.

Within the very *fact of father-hood* are stored away vast worlds of truth about God's Fatherhood, having little or no connection with the godliness or cruelty by which a given man expresses it.

Because Fatherhood is the central life, the central love, the central energy, the central meaning of the universe, and the most

> **WITHIN THE VERY *FACT OF FATHERHOOD* ARE STORED AWAY VAST WORLDS OF TRUTH ABOUT GOD'S FATHERHOOD.**

important truth for His creatures to grasp if they are to know life, God established the universe to function in such a way that a smaller kind of fatherhood, a picture of His own, would reside at the center of human life.

He thus ordained "fathers" and "mothers" as the procreators of earthly existence, passing on life and love to their offspring. He went to great lengths to explain to parents how they were to function in this role and accomplish the task He had set before them.

The whole process of earthly fatherhood and motherhood and childhood was to combine in such a way as to create a magnificent threefold portrait of the Godhead, of our heavenly Maker and Creator, and of the Fatherhood that gives life to everything in the universe.

As in all things, sin interrupted and corrupted the process. The enemy infiltrated the family unit, discrediting the earthly model of God's establishing. Instead of pointing us *to* God our Father, the incompleteness of earthly fatherhood has, with satan's help, embittered sons and daughters *against* their parents and, in so doing, blinded them to the magnificence of God's Fatherhood.

Thus has been dulled almost beyond recognition the essential human instinct—that created yearning to look up and behold our Father.

A gigantic stone sits in the middle of the road preventing each one of us from even thinking clearly on the subject, let alone getting past the obstacle.

For my sons, it is I, their earthly father.

For me, it's my father.

You have your *own* stone in the person of *your* father.

I tell my own sons: I am a woefully imperfect vessel for carrying such a lofty and marvelous truth—that God loves them utterly and completely and is doing everything in His creative power to reveal that love in mutual relationship with them.

As much as I love my sons, I don't love them *utterly*. I am a flawed, selfish, incomplete, imperfect human being. Compared with God's love, mine is a meager demonstration indeed. I am subject to the full range of human tendencies that obstruct love being fully felt, fully expressed, and fully lived out between men and women, parents and children, brothers and sisters, friends and acquaintances.

We were put on this earth to love, but none of us know how to do it very well. The earthly image of fatherhood, designed to show us how, is flawed.

It is an imperfect vessel.

17

LOOKING BEYOND...
TO PERFECT FATHERHOOD

IF EARTHLY FATHERS ARE INTENDED AS MIRRORS REFLECTING BACK some image of God, there is no denying they are cracked and broken. The image they reflect is incomplete and distorted.

There are millions of broken mirrors in the world, including the one each of us was born gazing into. Yet we still have to find our true Father.

The trouble is, many people, seeing that the mirror is broken or shattered, and embittered by whatever their own experience has been, turn their backs and walk away, never to discover God's Fatherhood at all.

> IT WAS NEVER THE ROLE OF EARTHLY FATHERS AND MOTHERS TO OFFER OTHER THAN PARTIAL IMAGES.

In fact it was never the role of earthly fathers and mothers to offer other than partial images. They yield but a portrayal of God's Fatherhood, in the same way that a tree or the sky or the seasons or a fragrant rose produce true but *partial* pictures of certain aspects of God's nature.

The common fallacy is to equate the fatherhood of one's earthly father with an accurate representation of God's heavenly Fatherhood. Though not intentionally, or even consciously, we draw this equal sign in our mistaken equation at a deep subconscious level very early in life.

However, as life progresses and we grow and learn, we fail to mature in this most vital area—we fail to learn the skills of higher spiritual mathematics necessary to undo that false human computation. The fatherhood equation must be rewritten. Yet it takes high-mountain vision to figure out the algebra of the divine formula.

Earthly fatherhood is intended only as a temporary enclosure for something far, far greater (that it is God's intent for all to seek and ultimately discover)—the perfection of Fatherhood we find in Him!

Once we allow the lives of our earthly fathers to carry out the work for which they were intended—imperfect and incomplete, yet pointing upward, causing us to ask, "Where is *perfect* and *complete* Fatherhood?"—then (and only then) are we ready to scale the heights toward the highestmost regions of the Fatherhood of our heavenly Father.

O God, reveal truth to us at this moment! Let us put away the smallness of our responses. Holy Spirit, we ask You to blow away the clouds that obscure our vision with cramped images of past hurts and disappointments. Show us the divine interrelation between fatherhood and Fatherhood. Teach us what father means as well as Father. Help us progress along these high pathways of our journey, ever deeper into the mountains toward Your presence. Give us eyes to see truth.

Help us to forgive our earthly fathers for their inadequacies, realizing their own humanness, so that we might walk through the doorway of forgiveness into the land of Your vast Fatherness.

O God, the cry of our hearts is that we might look beyond the imperfection of this life to the perfection of the love You have for us.

18

FATHERHOOD REQUIRES CHILDNESS

WHAT DOES IT MEAN, THAT WE MAY COME TO GOD with personal and familial address, that we can look upward, seeking His face, and call Him by that most private and confidential word, *Father*—and even the more intimate *Abba!*—as if there were only the two of us in all the universe? Of what is this intimacy comprised?

What prevents even diligent seekers from apprehending this central theme of the gospel story, causing them to satisfy their spiritual hungers with lesser meat? What so obscures the vision even of God's spiritual offspring from perceiving with clarity that which was the guiding truth of Jesus' every moment?

If the instinct exists within the men and women of God's making to look *up* to Fatherhood, why do they so often, like the animals, seek horizontal fulfillment only? Why do they turn their eyes away from that very thing for which their spirits yearn?

The answer to this pivotal question can be stated with far more simplicity than its truth can be translated into life. It is this: There can be no fatherhood without corresponding *childness*.

To acknowledge God as Father requires that I acknowledge myself as His child. Acknowledge that there is One above me, One who will *always*

63

be above me—older than me, bigger than me, wiser than me…infinite where I am finite, eternal where I am temporal, Creator where I am merely created. In every way the brain can imagine, He is the More, I am the less. He is the Initiator, I can only respond. I am utterly, unconditionally, and in all ways His *child*.

My reliance upon Him is total. I cannot live, cannot love, cannot think, cannot feel, cannot reason, cannot choose, cannot create apart from His Spirit breathing life through me. It is a relationship of dependence that I will never outgrow.

The very notion of self-rule is dead altogether.

The *Godness*, *authority*, and supreme *masculinity* of Fatherhood merge into a finality of overlordship from which there is not even the possibility of escape…ever. Ultimate Fatherhood is eternally over us.

Such are the components, the chemical formula, of the blue mountain air above the gray valley clouds. It goes against everything valley society has ingrained into us and everything we would prefer to believe.

The man or woman who resists this overarching truth by which the universe hangs together, holding out the vain and impossibly foolish fantasy that we may exist somehow out from under it, is destined to a life of constantly bumping against the painfully pricking goads of attempted self-reliance and self-rule.

When we identify God as Father, however, it is not a relationship of dependence that is begrudgingly acknowledged, it is one joyfully *welcomed*. Then first do we understand the overlordship of the universe. Recognizing the masculinity, the authority, and the Godness of divine

> RECOGNIZING THE MASCULINITY, THE AUTHORITY, AND THE GODNESS OF DIVINE FATHERHOOD, WE MUST *CHOOSE* TO WALK IN OUR CHILDNESS IN SUBMISSION TO THE FATHER.

Fatherhood, we must *choose* to walk in our childness in submission to the Father.

If the greatest stumbling block to recognizing the magnificence of God's Fatherhood is earthly fatherhood, then the greatest stumbling block to intimacy with the Father Himself is the *independence* every human soul craves.

Independence: *I am my own...I need none other.*

Here is the great barrier to the fulfillment of our destiny, the world's single great evil, the cause of all unhappiness abroad in the land, and the source of all frustrations and anxieties and that nagging sense dogging the heels that life is somehow not all it ought to be.

Independence. It is the great lie of the universe. It is what turned satan into the enemy of God's every purpose. In his heart, the power of love became the love of power. It is the inbred orientation that sits at stark odds with the one necessity of vertical significance—bowing before One greater.

Independence says: *I will be no one's child. Childness—ha! I outgrew that years ago! I am an independent entity, sufficient unto myself. I will not submit. No one will tell me what to do. I am my own master. I will call no one Father.*

Without acknowledged childness, intimacy with Fatherhood is impossible.

Though childness is required, however, it is not an attitude toward Him even the Father can *make* us adopt. He will never *force* any knee to bow before Him. Do we believe that Philippians 2:10 is literally true? The Greek *kampto* (καμπτω), which Paul uses as "to bend," indicates a chosen, willing, and worshipful veneration, not one of coercion. Our knees bend and our hands raise in humility and submission...only when we choose it.

Such acceding, such a laying down of self-rule, such a willing abandonment of one's life into the hands of Another is brought about by a decision. Engaging the will into chosen harmony with our Maker brings the mind, heart, and soul into alignment behind it.

Thus, if we are kept from the very intimacy we long for, if we do not make closer approach to that Fatherhood toward which our instinct draws us, if we do not drink of that water with which our soul thirsts to be satisfied, if we refuse to reach toward that high destiny that is the home in which our heart was made to dwell...we do so by our own choice.

Father, help us to see that You are not some cruel celestial taskmaster determined to pin us under Your thumb. Help us to recognize this most deadly of all snares masterminded by a society whose granaries of truth have gone bankrupt—that independence leads to happiness.

May we recognize the rightness, the truth, and the contentment inherent within a full interactive dependence upon the Father of Jesus Christ, as we extend our quest into the uppermost regions whence spring the only wells of fulfillment to be found in creation!

19

CREATION OF THE UNIVERSAL FAMILY

WHAT WE ARE TO APPREHEND FROM OUR FIRST IMAGES of human fatherhood is a foundational lesson. It is so simple, in fact, that it escapes most of humankind.

It is just this: Where there is an imperfect reflection, there must be a *perfect* Source of the reflection. It is a fact of the universe—every reflection has a source.

If there is an *incomplete* fatherhood, there must be a *perfect* Fatherhood. Therefore, if I am to be a true man or woman, I must seek to find that true Source, that *higher* Fatherhood.

What prevents God's creatures from entering into that happiest, that highest, that most wonderful and holy relationship that He intended?

Society and modernity, certainly, pressure against it.

The self-motivated will of man, of course, makes choices contrary to it.

And sin infiltrates every corner of man's being with the lie of independence, that most serious of all preventative inoculations to ward off intimacy.

But let's get more personal. Let's stop talking about "man" and "mankind." What prevents *you* and *me* from laying hold of the very relationship everything within us cries out for?

This question probes the very bedrock of our spiritual existence. To find the answer requires journeying back toward the distant foundations of all things—back to the very beginning in Genesis 1—back to the sixth day of creation.

Let us seek there, not abstract history, but truth for ourselves. For what purpose did God create man on that significant sixth day of creation?

Who among His fallen world of creatures can probe the infinitely ageless, creatively motivated heart of God? His infinitude is unknowable by our finiteness. To ask *why* God does anything is rendered contradictory by definition. He is not subject to the *whys* of reason.

> **GOD *IS*,
> THEREFORE...
> *EVERYTHING*!**

God *is*, therefore...*everything*!

What He wills simply is. I AM is His name. No *why* fits into that I-AM-ness.

He delights, however, when we apply ourselves more deeply to understand His ways, seeking not the contradictory *whys* of man's convoluted reasonings, but eager to enter into the *divine whys* of the Father's plan.

Let us thus dare suggest the following: God created man to expand the family of His Fatherness.

The expression of the Son within the Godhead was a holy extension of the divine Being. But the Son was an "only child." And the creative heart of Love beat with creating love-energy toward more sons and daughters whom He could bring into His family as brothers and sisters to His Son.

"Let *Us* make man in *Our* image," God said.[1] The divine family—the threefold *Us*—already walked the earth prior to day six, but the Father of that triune family desired more creatures to partake in it.

They would be of a lesser nature, it is true, and far more vulnerable. To give them the greatest gift possible—the free will of mortal choice—would involve an enormous risk. But the divine Firstborn would be their elder Brother. He would help them learn to live in their childness within the family of creation, even sacrificing for them if need be. He would be all an elder

Brother should be. And in spite of their potential susceptibility to forces outside the family, they would still retain the image of their Creator-Father. His fingerprint could never be eradicated from their hearts.

So the Father created man, and His universal family was made. And He blessed them, giving them dominion and wisdom and food and companionship and pleasure and the most wondrous place imaginable to live.

He created these younger brothers and sisters to fellowship with Him and His Firstborn, to walk with them in the Garden in the cool of the day, to work the earth of His creation, to reproduce, to tend the lower creatures of His unbounded divine imagination, to rule the earth, and to fully enjoy all the goodness He had made.

Everything God made was good...including His children.

God saw that it was good.

God saw that it was good!

God saw that it was *good*!!

So vital and significant is this truth of goodness that God instructed the writer of the Genesis account to repeat it seven times—the number of perfection—punctuating it after the creation of man with the words *very good.*

Goodness was the air of the Garden. And it is the oxygen we must learn to breathe if we are to travel far in the mountainous regions of faith. As familiar as we are with the word, however, living by the vitality and life-energy of its sustenance is unfamiliar. The valley theologians to whom we have long listened have corrupted the word, and made us afraid to imagine that God might be *too* good. As a result, we don't imagine Him good enough.

This is the resounding truth of Genesis 1: "God created man in His own image...God saw all that He had made, and it was very good. And there was evening, and there was morning—the sixth day."[2]

Incredible as it seems, there is a certain branch of pietism and populist theology prevalent today that speaks of some of the old-fashioned scriptural virtues, such as goodness, as if they are actually bad things. This short-sightedness isolates a verse such as Isaiah 64:6—"All of us have become like one who is unclean, and all our righteous acts are like filthy rags"—and erects an entire theology around it, ignoring the sevenfold declaration of Genesis *from God's own mouth.* Misguided doctrines result, putting black above white, making hell a deeper truth in the economy of eternity than God's victory, and declaring the starting point for the gospel to be sin instead of love.

Those who make sin the foundational starting point for attempting to understand the nature of man do God's creation a grievous wrong. With that sand-built base as their starting point, they are able to understand neither man nor the Father. Rather than undergird their theologies with the eternal bedrock of Genesis 1—the beginning!—they begin their erroneous expositions at Genesis 3, as if the *very good* declaration of the Creator did not even exist.

They come at truth from the wrong angle altogether, thus entirely missing the vital point that *goodness lies deeper in the heart of man's nature than the sin, which came later, and entered from the outside.*

Goodness lies deeper in man because God put Himself there. It was *very* good!

Goodness is intrinsic to man's nature. Sin is not. Sin is the corrupting virus that has temporarily contaminated goodness. But even sin itself cannot alter the truth of Genesis 1:31 that echoes throughout all eternity.

Goodness lies deep in the bedrock of the universe, not merely because what God created was good, but because goodness embodies God's nature itself.

Do we seek to know what the Father is like? We have not far to look. We have only to open our Bibles and read one chapter—the very first chapter. *Good, good, good, good, good, good...very good!*

The divine fingerprint of what He created reflects who God is at every point! Perfect (sevenfold) goodness.

Following the mighty creation of Genesis 1 came the triumphant unveiling of God's ultimate and perfect blueprint of life within His newly created family—the majestic glory of Genesis 2. Here was *life* as God intended it—*good* life!

Genesis 2 details perfection. It opens with rest, with a holy day, because creation was fully accomplished...and fully good. It goes on to describe the kind of life God intended to enjoy with His creatures. A beautiful Garden was to be their home. Trees were planted that were pleasing to look at and with fruit pleasing to eat.

What provision! Not mere trees, but good and pleasing trees. Not just some trees...*all* kinds of trees!

Did Adam and Eve *need* to eat of the tree of the knowledge of good and evil? Of course not. They had every other kind of tree imaginable, as well as every other generous provision.

It was an enormous Garden. Four mighty rivers flowed through it. The very word *Garden* may give us an entirely limited impression. For all we know, this Garden where God dwelt with man could have comprised the entire Middle East...or perhaps half the globe.

Life with God in the Garden was anything but dull. It was a life of constantly receiving good from the hands of God.

God gave and gave and gave...and everything He gave was very good!

He gave Adam a helper, Eve. He gave both of them all they needed. He gave them the privilege of working with Him to tend the Garden.

He gave them food. He gave them freedom. He gave them pleasure. He gave them wisdom and knowledge. He gave them dominion over the earth. He gave them innocence.

Most of all, He gave them fellowship with Himself, the God who had made them.

He gave them nothing less than a *perfect* life.

Perfection everywhere!

How long they lived in the Garden in this perfect and innocent state it is impossible to conjecture, but it clearly went on for an extended period—time enough for Adam to name *all* the birds and *all* the beasts of the ground.

We sometimes imagine that the fall occurred within 24 hours of the creation of man. I don't think so. This innocent state of life might have lasted a hundred years or more for all we know.

Genesis 2 is one of the Bible's most significant chapters, offering limitless insight into the purposes of God's heart!

ENDNOTES

1. Gen. 1:26 NIV.
2. Gen. 1:27,31 NIV.

20

THE FIRST LIE OF GENESIS 3

AFTER THE CREATION OF GOD'S UNIVERSAL FAMILY, the enemy corrupted its goodness with the evil virus called sin.

Two lies, following the pride of satan's rebellion, were sent to enter man's brain...and sunder him from his Creator.

The first we have already spoken of. It is still with us, and daily continues its dissevering work. Its evil name is *independence*. Though I call it a name, I will not venerate the lie with the upper case.

"Did God really say you could not eat?" his treacherous tongue whispers. "Nah, you mustn't bother about that. You don't *need* God. You can live without Him."

The lie of independence.

The lie that broke and destroyed the innocent *childness* of life in the Garden.

No more insidious and perfect lie could have been sent to destroy the Genesis 2 relationship between the Father and His created children.

FATHERHOOD *REQUIRES* CHILDNESS

How lethal is the spirit of independence, absolutely preventing a right and humble child's heart before Fatherhood. Indeed, where independence reigns, Fatherhood itself becomes impossible.

Fulfilled Fatherhood *requires* childness—requires looking up and outside ourselves for direction to life.

True childness *requires* submission to One greater—submission given by willing, self-denying choice. Such was Adam and Eve's Garden life in Genesis 2.

Submission born of coercion is no submission at all. True childness is entered into by the full and happy choice of the child himself.

I will not be my own, says such a one. I have no desire to be my own.

I WILL to belong to another.

I CHOOSE not to be master of my own fate and destiny.

I WANT never to be independent about anything again.

I MAKE myself a child for the rest of my days.

I DECIDE to ask my Father what He would have of me.

I DESIRE to say, think, do, plan, hope for nothing but what the Father would want me to say, think, do, plan, or hope.

I ACCEPT that the Father knows what is best for me in ways far beyond my own capacity to know what is best.

I LAY DOWN all claim to independence, that my Father might be all to me. Henceforth, I am wholly and utterly, in all ways, His child.

Fatherhood and independence are mutually exclusive. Neither can exist in the presence of the other.

Because young children have no choice but to live under the authority of and, in a sense, in submission to their parents, it is easy to assume that they are "children" in the full and proper sense.

Not so.

They are offspring. They have been placed within families as children, occupying the role of children, in order to be trained in the most elemental lesson in all the universe—that lesson which all men and women must one day learn: To *trust*, so that they might desire to become *true children* indeed.

Alas, how very few learn to apprehend this foundational necessity for happiness and fulfillment!

In truth, the spirit of independence reigns more thoroughly within the heart of a human child than in any other place within the created kingdom of planet Earth. It is this independence that the God-ordained and Heaven-established family order was intended to purge out of him, that he might desire to put independence behind him and enter into a life with true *Fatherhood*, of which the earthly motherhood and fatherhood of his parents are but a faint and broken echo.

There is a childness into which we must all learn to grow, as well as a childhood we must all leave behind.

The latter we cannot help. There is no other way to come into being than as offspring of human parents. This process we share with the animal kingdom. But that unique calling of the divine within us, that instinct to cast our gaze upward, such is the stamp of God Himself upon our nature.

It is the call to become *His children*!

That is a childness that can only be entered into by the willing, submitted, self-denying choice to lay the independence of earthly childhood forever aside.

It is a childness of maturity. It represents the apex, the flowering of the human plant, the very pinnacle of life's development.

To this choice, to this *growth into childness*, the earthly family—with its fatherhood, its motherhood, and its childhood—has forever been intended to lead. That it does help so few children to grow into childness is sad indication that so few of its fathers and mothers are children of divine childness themselves.

Independence blocks the path to childness. It was the first lie told to man, and it has been preventing Fatherhood ever since.

21

THE SECOND LIE
OF GENESIS 3

THE INSTANT THE LIE OF INDEPENDENCE WAS SWALLOWED, with the first disobedient action of man—the bite from the fruit of the tree—the second lie immediately entered the brain of man to compound the result of his disobedience a hundredfold.

Independence led to disobedience. But man's fall from fellowship with God was not yet absolute. His fate, indeed, the entire history of the world, hung in the balance. Even after disobeying, Adam and Eve might still have remained in fellowship with God...*if* they had responded in childship.

A new choice was suddenly before them. How would they respond to what they had done? What would they do?

Then the new lie spoke into their ears. They turned...and listened.

The evil name of the second lie was *fear.* This lie was equally insidious—and even more subtle.

"Have you sinned?" it whispered. "Then God is going to punish you. Hide from Him! It is your only chance."

Ah, the subtlety of its lying tongue! Replete, as are all lies from the enemy, with enough half-truth to masquerade as truth.

Even more easily than they believed the first, Adam and Eve now swallowed the second. Instantly they ceased to be the wise children of innocent childlikeness, and became instead immature children of *childishness*.

They abandoned childness. They tried, foolish in their childish *independence*, to cover their nakedness. Then they attempted to hide from God Himself, cowering in this newfound sensation called *fear*.

Foolish children!

Did you truly sin? Then perhaps your Father will have to punish you in order to train you. But He is still your Father, and greater is His love than His disappointment that you have not obeyed Him.

There is but one course open to you.

Run *to* Him, not away from Him!

Do not hesitate. *He is your refuge* against these lies.

Seek His help. Throw yourselves into the embrace of your Father! Tearfully confess to Him your foolishness. Step back again into the childness in which you were created to live.

> **RUN *TO* HIM. DO NOT HESITATE. *HE IS YOUR REFUGE.***

Become again His children!

It is your only chance.

Fear changes only two words from the full and glorious truth of our salvation! *Run to* Him becomes *hide from* Him...lie of lies!

What might the loving Father have done had Adam gone straight to Him with confession and repentance, learning his lesson from believing the first lie sufficiently to enable him to reject the second?

Discipline from the Father's hand would still have been rendered. Perhaps the gate to the Garden still would have been closed. Oh, but how different thereafter might have been the fellowship between the Father and His family!

What restoration might have it been in the Father's heart to extend had the first Adam offered to make himself also the second, saying to his Maker,

"Father, I have sinned. I have disobeyed Your command. I was foolish to do so. I am sorry. The woman is blameless, for You gave me to rule over her. I take account for all. Take my life, for I deserve nothing less, and spare her. Let the whole of Your punishment fall upon me. Be it unto me according to Your will."

But none of this was to be.

The lie of fear had gained a foothold from which it would never retreat. And the lie that our Father is to be feared persists today, still poisoning our capacity to correctly discern God's Fatherhood, preventing us from looking into His face, barring the way to intimacy.

The glory of Genesis 2 was undone.

22

ALL THE WAY BACK TO THE GARDEN

Is HARSH DISCIPLINARY FATHERHOOD ANYWHERE NEAR the *source* of Creation?

Do we see it in Genesis 1? Is it to be found in the interactive life within the Garden of Genesis 2, where the Creator and His family fellowshiped and walked together—ruling, procreating, growing, and working—according to the Father's purpose?

No. It came later.

But not until Genesis 3—not until God's purposes and plan had been laid out and established for all to see.

Then the corrupting lies of independence and fear entered, changing the equation of life forever.

However, in the Father's infinite love, the power of these lies has been broken, and the breach caused by the sundering curse healed. The firstborn Son went to the Father to do what the first Adam could not, saying, "Let it fall upon Me, that My younger brothers and sisters might live. Bring them back to the Garden. Reinstate them to their position in our family, that they might again have fellowship with You, their Father and Mine."

Those who call themselves Christians, therefore, no longer need live under the curse of sin, separation from God, subject to the enemy's lies.

Jesus revealed the lies for what they are, and defeated satan's power over us forever.

Those who follow Him, and trust Him are "taken backward," in a sense, through a spiritual time machine (if such a metaphor can be brought to our aid without demeaning the imperative of the principle) *into the relationship with the Father that existed prior to the Fall.* The apparatus for the accomplishment of this majestic purpose is described in Ephesians 4:8— "When He ascended on high, He led captives in His train."

Having sinned, and recognizing the "wages" of that sin, we are allowed to be cleansed of it and to stand before the Father blameless, guiltless, robed in white.

Such a wonderful and ingenious provision has been made for us by both Father and Son. In spite of our sin, we have been reinstated into the family of God. The Garden fellowship of Genesis 2 is still ours to enjoy.

We can become His children again!

The Prodigal Son parable of Luke 15 precisely describes the process: We had it all. We chose to go away and leave everything our Father had provided. To do so was foolish and landed us in despair. However, we may return home. The Father is waiting with open arms and a smile on His face. We have only to admit our foolishness...and become again His children.

Jesus was talking about us!

Unknowingly, however, most of us accept Christ's atonement but partially. We dabble His blood scantily upon the doorposts of our hearts, just sufficiently to ward off the angel of death. But we do not wash our entire selves in the full redemptive power of that blood, sufficient to fully reinstate us into the life of God's family of Genesis 2.

We continue instead to listen to the twin lies.

Though having experienced the second birth, which Jesus spoke of as the doorway into this spiritual time machine, we still try to do what Adam could not—live in what we call fellowship with God while remaining fundamentally independent of His Fatherhood in our life.

In other words, positionally we have "gone back" to the Garden...but not quite all the way back. We have gone back only far enough to enable us to scrape out an existence between Genesis 3:13 and Genesis 3:14.

We have gone back past the curse. Thank God we are free of that! Praise the Lord for the atoning blood of Jesus. Sin no longer has eternal power over us. The angel of death has seen the blood and passed over.

But we have not gone back *past* the lies of independence and fear that spoke in Genesis 3:4 and 3:10. Those, we're still listening to. They clog our ears and blind our eyes with their lies, still obscuring the Father from us, just as they did to Adam's vision.

We have not killed the power of independence by choosing to submit in childness to life with the Father. We continue to heed the lie—*I alone have the right to be master of my life.*

You can have your sins forgiven and go back to Genesis 3...and still be in fellowship with the serpent and his two lying demons.

Strong words, perhaps, when they fall upon complacent ears—yet true.

Jesus' mission on earth, the reason for the Cross and the purpose for which He descended and then rose with captives in His train, was to take those captives of sin all the way back into *full* fellowship and life with His Father! *All the way back* to Genesis 2...to life in the Father's family *before* the lies. Unless we get back to Genesis 2,

> JESUS' MISSION ON EARTH WAS TO TAKE THOSE CAPTIVES OF SIN ALL THE WAY BACK INTO *FULL* FELLOWSHIP AND LIFE WITH HIS FATHER! *ALL THE WAY BACK* TO GENESIS 2.

we cannot truly experience intimacy with the Father. Independence and fear will keep us from knowing Him rightly.

Applying the brakes and getting off the train of Jesus' ascent prematurely at Genesis 3:13 may get us what is called "saved," and thus qualify us for entry into Heaven on the first round. But getting off there will not accomplish the purpose for which Jesus came, for which He died, for which He bore us in His train back to the Father's heart.

The only way for that to be accomplished is to go the full distance with our elder Brother, the firstborn Son—all the way back to the Garden life of Genesis 2. All the way back—beyond the lies and the fig leaves of fear—into the very arms of our loving Father!

Such is the pinnacle, the mountaintop, of the Christian faith.

23

LOOKING BEYOND FEAR

MOST OF OUR MISTAKEN NOTIONS AND MISUNDERSTANDINGS concerning God begin with fear. We've kept fear front and center in our incorrect Fatherhood equation.

Fear of God is the chief cause of our unbelief. More than any other single factor, it keeps us from knowing the Father intimately.

After the Cross, fear is to be no more. The lies have been unmasked, their power broken. Paul wrote to Timothy: "God has not given us a spirit of fear."[1] He is not a Father to be hidden from, run from, or feared.

Despite knowing this truth as well as we do, most of us continue allowing the lying rascal to hang around, misting over our vision with fog from the low places whenever we try to look up toward the Father's face.

Now it is true that the Bible says that "the fear of the Lord is the beginning of wisdom."[2] However, we don't understand what a right and proper fear of the Lord is. Thus, instead of it bringing us wisdom and intimacy with the Father, it keeps us from both.

Fear, to the earthbound senses, results from something terrifying or painful. Fear of God as felt by most, fills us with the gnawing sense that He is waiting to pounce when we do wrong. Punishment is the inevitable result. Nagging images of Dante's hell contribute to this incorrect equation. Even Christians, knowing that hell is out there somewhere, even if perhaps not for them, allow it to miscolor their vision of the Father as a celestial policeman,

85

judge, prison warden, and grim, unflinching torturer of the wicked. Beginning from a wrong perspective, how can our approach to God be anything but timid and fearful?

This is the same lie that fear first told Adam in Genesis 3, "God is going to level His wrath on you the minute He sees you! *Hide from Him! It's your only chance.*" And we're still listening.

We've got the formula of Fatherhood incorrect. The minute we do wrong, we make *God* the enemy who is after us, rather than embracing Him as our salvation and refuge from the true enemy—our sin. We don't know our Father very well. Nor do we know how properly to "fear" Him.

Fear can be a normal and healthy thing. God placed fear inside us. He put it there for our protection.

Before he can swim, a child's natural fear of the water protects him from drowning. But once he has learned to swim, that fear is replaced by the capacity to fully enjoy the water, along with a respect for it. He knows, appreciates, and understands the water, its power, even its danger. But he is no longer frightened of it, nor afraid to venture near it.

In the absence of any other response to God, fear is a useful place to begin. Fear is rudimentary, a beginning, a response of childhood, but something that is cast aside when spiritual adulthood comes.

Fear of punishment is likewise a response of spiritual childhood—useful for training as far as it goes, but unable to guide you more than a step or two along the path.

The fear of God *is* the beginning of wisdom. Better to fear God than ignore Him.

Disobeying God indeed does bring fearsome consequences. A lifetime's independence from Him, a lifetime spent ignoring the calls of His voice, a lifetime spent pleasing only oneself, a lifetime's disobedience of His commands, a lifetime's sin...we do well to tremble at the consequences of such foolishness.

What we need to fear, however, is the consequences of sin, not the Father who can rescue us from that sin altogether.

Adam's initial response was correct. He had sinned. He did well to fear.

The fear, however, ought to have been directed at his disobedience, and what it indicated about his own heart, not toward the Father. Given what he had done, his Father was his only refuge from what was inside him. His own rebellion was the enemy, not God.

Hell awaits those who persist in ignoring God. But they should not fear their Father. *He* is their salvation.

There are two kinds of fear—God's and the devil's.

The fear that properly encourages us toward relationship with our Father is the fear of Genesis 2—a fear established by God's design, the loving awe with which we are to honor, respect, and obey Him. Such fear is indeed the beginning of wisdom.

"Obey Me," says our Father, "so that you will know life. Walk with Me and all I have made is yours."

Genesis 3 fear, on the other hand, came not from the loving Father's heart, but from the twisted and prideful heart of the enemy. *Hide from Him!* says the lie. *If He finds you, He will kill you.*

> WHY ARE WE SO RELUCTANT TO ACCEPT THE IMAGE OF THE FATHER THAT JESUS HIMSELF GAVE?

If we live in Genesis 3—fearful *of* God—how will we ever learn to walk *with* Him in the coolness of the day? If the lie of fear builds the house of our faith, how can God's Fatherhood find a home within us? If the bricks in the walls of our spiritual abodes are mortared together with hide-from-Him fear, how can they withhold the lying whispers of the enemy?

Why are we so reluctant to accept the image of the Father that Jesus Himself gave? What would have been God's response had Adam run to Him instead of fleeing in fear...run to Him to confess his wrong?

We know what it would have been. Did not Jesus Himself tell us in Luke 15:18-23?

> *"I will set out and go back to my father and say to him: Father, I have sinned against heaven and against you. I am no longer worthy to be called your son...." So he got up and went to his father. But while he was still a long way off, his father saw him and was filled with compassion for him; he ran to his son, threw his arms around him and kissed him....But the father said to his servants, "Quick! Bring the best robe and put it on him. Put a ring on his finger and sandals on his feet. Bring the fattened calf and kill it. Let's have a feast and celebrate."*

Fear is only the beginning of wisdom.

Oh, God our Father, why are we so hesitant to accept You as Jesus described You? Open our eyes to see the exuberant and unreserved love of Your Fatherhood! Let us fear our sin, but never You. And may that fear send us running straight into Your loving arms.

ENDNOTES

1. See 2 Tim. 1:7.
2. Ps. 111:10; Prov. 9:10 NIV.

24

GOD'S PURPOSE—INTIMACY, NOT PUNISHMENT

A SIGNIFICANT WEIGHT WE MUST LEAVE BEHIND IN SCALING THE HEIGHTS to reacquaint ourselves with God and know Him aright is this: Knowing the Father may begin with fear, but to know Him intimately, the lie of improper fear must be banished. Only then can be established a right and proper Genesis 2 relationship between child and Father.

A deadly misunderstanding infects humankind—the assumption that God's first and most important business is to punish those who do wrong. It remains one of the most grievous sources of fatal thinking extant in the land. Christians are among those *most* bound by it. They've gotten off Jesus' reverse salvation train at Genesis 3:13, where the lies of independence and fear still swirl about.

But it is all wrong.

The Father's primary purpose is to reestablish the intimacy of Genesis 2 with His creation. If punishment is occasionally necessary to accomplish this end, it is a tool He will use. But punishment is not His *primary* purpose.

Why do we think wrongly about God's intent? Why do theologians insist that God's *holiness* cannot have anything to do with us in our sinful state?

Because fear is part of our makeup. We are Adam's offspring. The lie he believed is still being whispered in our ears every day.

The elders of our traditions have built upon the lie, erecting huge doctrinal edifices upon it, solemnly intoning that punishment of sin is God's chief end in the universe, and probably His sole interest in us as well. They turn truths that are necessary as wall-supports of faith—fear of sin's consequences—into foundations. There's nothing wrong with the construction materials. They've just got them in the wrong place.

We've got fear pointed in the wrong direction—toward the Father instead of toward sin.

> WE'VE GOT FEAR POINTED IN THE WRONG DIRECTION— TOWARD THE FATHER INSTEAD OF TOWARD SIN.

Today's populist theologians and evangelists have learned to couch the above in agreeable ways, double-talking their way into the pleasant-sounding illusion that they are making God's love and goodness supreme. However, at the heart, if followed to their logical end point and deepest conclusions, many Christian belief systems are founded on a response to the punishment that God is required by His nature to mete out upon sinners.

They're still listening to the evil whisper: *Hide from Him! It's your only chance.*

They bring Jesus in as the refuge and "hiding place," but the effect is still the same. *Flee from the wrath that is to come!*

Flee *from* God. Flee *to* Jesus. The *Son* will protect and save us from the Father!

How both Jesus and His Father must be grieved to see how we have twisted their loving Genesis 2 relationship to fit our Genesis 3 *hide-from-Him* theologies.

A right and proper Genesis 2 relationship with the Father does not exclude loving discipline from His hand. The Bible says He disciplines those He loves. What obedient son or daughter of an eternal Father would desire it otherwise? We *want* to grow. How else but through discipline when

90

we require it? But He should not have to come find us when we need discipline, asking, as He did of Adam and Eve, "Where are you?"

If His loving discipline is needed, the faithful child should already be running swiftly toward Him even before He calls!

25

A God to Call Father

WHEN WE LEAVE THE LIE OF FEAR BEHIND, A WHOLE NEW WORLD of revelation opens into the Father's being.

Everything in life mirrors and reflects deeper principles in God's Kingdom. All the hidden clues of discovery we spoke about earlier are clues about Him. He made every inch of the world, every plant, every thorn on every rose bush, every petal, every tree, every blade of grass.

They all reflect something about God's personality...if we have eyes to see the hidden mysteries of meaning!

Once we're able to look above the valley fogs, a huge truth becomes visible. Lay hold of it, and the discovery will be such an adventure that your life will never be the same again!

The most important mystery in life is this: *God is our Father.*

He is a Father whose great desire is not to punish us for doing wrong, but to reveal Himself to us, His children. And then to live with us in intimacy.

> HE IS A FATHER WHOSE GREAT DESIRE IS NOT TO PUNISH US FOR DOING WRONG, BUT TO REVEAL HIMSELF TO US, HIS CHILDREN.

He wants us to know Him as a loving and kind and generous and giving Father who delights in His children knowing Him. He wants to walk and visit and fellowship and converse with us in a growing friendship of love.

He is approachable, not distant.

He does not want us to think of Him primarily as the Awful Powerful Almighty Sovereign of the universe, Creator of the Heavens, Destroyer of sin.

He is all those, of course, and much more. There are thousands of aspects and attributes to His character.

But what He wants us to call Him is *Father*.

He wants us to go to Him so He can wrap His arms around us and speak to us tenderly and lovingly as His children.

Does it not sound particularly remarkable? We've been talking about this ever since we set out together.

Everybody knows the *words*, knows the *fact* of it.

But very few know how to walk in the Fatherness of that central truth. Why?

Because they're stuck at the point of improper fear—fearing God rather than the consequences of their sin. Therefore, they can't see what His Fatherhood truly entails. The distinction is between Genesis 3 "Christianity" versus vibrant Genesis 2 *intimacy*.

The Garden of Genesis 2, the divine and universal "familyhood" of the Creator—that's where He wants us to live...with Him!

He is a Father exactly as Jesus portrayed in Luke 15, with arms wide open, with a smile on His face, waiting to celebrate life with His creatures.

Jesus told that parable so that we would know what our Father is like! Such is the wonderful childness into which we may enter in friendship with Him.

We are all brothers and sisters, living on this earth together with a common purpose: To discover together as much about the Father as we can...and then to go to Him.

He is our Father, we are His children. Now we have to become *children of childness* by laying aside both our independence and fear.

He is not an angry Father, a cruel taskmaster, severe judge intent only on punishing us when we do wrong. He is a good Father, whose delight is in revealing His love to us.

He is the one good in all the world.

We delight in being with Him because He delights in us. And the more we are with Him, the more of His being and creation He reveals to us. He is our protector and our friend, our companion and Father—never more our fear.

He is a God to call *Father*.

Ah, Father, what delight You want us to take in finding You so close! Once we apprehend Your Fatherhood, how wonderful it is to realize that You are beside us every moment, and that such closeness is not fearsome. You want us to walk with You in the cool of the day, between You and Jesus. We need have no fear of You, but can delight in being in Your presence every moment. You are a Father anxious to smile with us, anxious to speak tenderly to us, anxious to hold us and protect us in Your arms.

26

JESUS DID NOT COME TO
SAVE US FROM THE FATHER

WHY DID JESUS COME TO EARTH?

Was it to save the world from its sins?

If so, why was it necessary for Jesus to save us from sin?

To keep us from an eternity in hell?

To answer *yes* makes avoiding hell and being saved from God's punishment the chief reason for the incarnation of Jesus upon the earth.

Now Jesus did die, of course, and He did atone for our sins and save us from hell. Such was intrinsic to the Father's purpose.

Such was not, however, His *central* purpose.

Sadly, a great many Christians view Jesus' mission to earth as being sent to protect us from certain death at the hand of an angry God intent upon the eternal punishment of sin and all "sinners" who die in that sin without having made a confession of Christ as Savior. Such is the prevailing evangelical interpretation of the Atonement and Jesus' death on the cross.

Though this is not explicitly stated, the implication is that Jesus saves us *from God* almost more than from our sins.

But God cannot be both loving Father and avenging Angel of Death at the same time. He can display a wide variety of seemingly disparate characteristics in His complex nature. But His intrinsic being must be *one*.

It's the dichotomy between Genesis 2 and Genesis 3. It's the chasm between Garden fellowship and the lie crying, *Hide!*

Jesus didn't come primarily to save us from the vengeful "hands of an angry God." He came to tell us:

Your sins are going to result in your death. But your Father loves you so much that He has sent Me to you, so that I could lead you back up to Him! I cannot Myself save you. I am merely the Son. I have come to rescue you and take you home. The Father has sent Me for you...because of His great love for you. He is your salvation and refuge. I am the one He sent to offer it to you. He alone, your tender and loving Father, can save you from your sins!

Come, take my hand, let Me show you your wonderful and loving Father. Don't hide from Him. Come to Him...with Me.

That was Jesus' purpose: To reveal God's personality and character, and to lead us to the Father, so that the Son and the Father *together* might save us from our sins.

God is our Father. Jesus came to show us and tell us what He is like. By pitting Jesus *against* the Father, as if

> ## GOD IS OUR FATHER. JESUS CAME TO SHOW US AND TELL US WHAT HE IS LIKE.

the Atonement were a gigantic shield that Jesus holds up to ward off the deadly arrows of the Father's wrath, is to erect a schism in the very center of the Godhead itself.

To our shame, this theology is based on a schizophrenic God who cannot Himself decide which half of His nature to direct toward earth—His hatred of sin, or His love for His creatures. And it is a heartbreaking oversimplification from the enemy, unknowingly deepened into the evangelical consciousness by its most popular preachers and theologians, who cannot imagine that God might perhaps be more forgiving than they.

God is triumphantly *one*. His nature *must* be one. And His nature is to love and forgive.

George MacDonald wrote, "God is one, and the depth of foolishness is reached by that theology which talks of God as if he held different offices and differed in each. It sets a contradiction in the very nature of God himself. It represents him as having to do something as a judge which as a father he would not do."[1]

The Atonement originates in the Father's *love*, not in His *vengeance*. Jesus was sent that the Father might *love* us back home with open arms, not *threaten* us back with a whip.

> *Father, forgive us for believing so comfortably the lies of fear, even more than we have believed in Your goodness. Forgive us for glossing over the words of Your Son: "I and the Father are one." Forgive us for erecting a schism in the Godhead of Your being, as if it were the Son's duty to protect us from the Father! Forgive us our foolish blindness that would pit Jesus against You!*
>
> *Thank You for opening our eyes to the truth that Jesus wants to take us to You, in whom is our salvation, not hide us from Your wrath behind His atonement. Forgive us for so long living in the midst of this dichotomy created by our unbelief.*
>
> *Help us to see, dear Father, that independence and fear— and all the lies satan sends against us—are the enemies we need to be saved from! Sin is the enemy, not our precious loving Father!*
>
> *Truly we need rescuing, and You are the one who can save us!*
>
> *Open our eyes still more, Father. Reveal more of the high purposes of Your truth to us. Help us to cast off the futile fig leaves of our fear, confessing ourselves the children we are. Surround us with the warmth of Your embrace.*
>
> *Help us to become fully mature sons and daughters.*

GOD: A GOOD FATHER

O God our Father, help us to believe in Your smiling, open-armed goodness!

ENDNOTE

1. George MacDonald, *Unspoken Sermons*, Third Series (London: Longmans, Green, & Co., 1889), 114-15.

27

HOW BIG IS OUR GOD?

TWO WORDS THAT REVEAL HOW BIG GOD'S FATHERHOOD IS, while at the same time prevent most people from fathoming a trillionth of its reality, are: *utterly* and *everything*.

Christians living in the low valleys of faith know that God loves them. They don't, however, really know in their hearts that He loves them *utterly*.

Valley Christians know in small measure that God does what He can to reveal His love and desires relationship with them. They are reluctant, however, to recognize that He will do *everything* possible to cause that to happen.

Noted British scholar, J.B. Phillips, wrote a book whose title contributes as much to the quest after Fatherhood as the content of the book: *How Big Is Your God?* Dozens of times I have turned those simple words upon myself, realizing that my faithlessness at some point stemmed from the fact that I was attempting to place my trust in a lowercase god.

How do I view the two words *utterly* and *everything*?

Do I *really* believe in an uppercase God? Does God love me *utterly*? Will God do *everything* possible to reveal that love?

How big is the God/god we trust and believe in?

What might be the implications if we took these words at face value and really believed that God not just loved us, but loved us *utterly*...that He not merely desires relationship with us, but can and will do *everything* to bring that about?

How BIG are we willing to believe God is?

Not only how big are we willing to believe, but how big might we *dare* think the Father is! Can we add courage to our faith? How far might we be bold enough to think His loving Fatherhood will extend?

> ## HOW BIG MIGHT WE *DARE* THINK THE FATHER IS!

Are we willing to use our imaginations to stretch faith toward the utter-everything-ness of His Fatherhood?

Some will be afraid to do so.

Yet God has not given us a spirit of fear, but of loving boldness!

The best way to learn of the Father is to listen to what Jesus said and then ask for His help. He is our elder Brother. This is the purpose for which He came to earth, and He eagerly awaits our asking. If Jesus came to show us the Father, then let us allow Him to do just that.

Spirit of Truth, Jesus our Brother, we ask for Your help in this quest. We have prayed for the Father to reveal Himself, to open the eyes of our heart and mind to see Him as He truly is. Now we ask You also to reveal truth to our innermost parts.

As we read of Your life on earth, illuminate the eyes of our understanding to see the Father's being and character in Your words, in what You did, in what You were constantly teaching Your disciples. Turn us to Your life, as written by Your servants Matthew, Mark, Luke, and John. Open our eyes to their words. Open us to the Fatherhood of their message.

O Lord our Savior and Friend, reveal to us more and more what You meant when You said that if we have seen You, we have seen the Father.

28

FOLLOW FATHERHOOD TO FINALITY

IF THE SONS AND DAUGHTERS OF GOD'S FAMILY FULLY APPREHENDED the simple fact that we could follow the Fatherhood of God all the way to finality, all the way back to a Genesis 2 relationship, the world may well have been redeemed centuries ago.

Men and women are so desperately hungry for true Fatherhood, and we children of His family have been entrusted to take it to them.

However, and sadly, *we* do not know the fullness of God's Fatherhood either. Saddest of all, many who live in His family are not hungry to discover it!

Before us, therefore, is the vital question: How do we break the shells and peel away the husks that enclose truths about God so that we can get all the way *inside* them, where dwells intimacy with the Father?

Discovery has to begin by following God's attributes out to the end to see what they really imply. That's how to find out if we *really* believe what we *say* we believe.

A key foundation stone in the writings of two of the last century's renowned exponents of the faith—Francis Schaeffer and C.S. Lewis—was their insistence that people must look at the logical conclusions of their own words: If I say I believe such-and-such, then what is the practical implication of that belief when it is followed all the way out to its ultimate and logical conclusion?

Logical-consequence thinking forces you to make a foundational evaluation concerning the veracity of your belief system. Can you, or can you not, *live* by your beliefs? Do they hold up when followed to the end?

If I live in the Sahara, for example I might say, "I do not believe that rain exists."

But what are the logical consequences of that belief when I travel to Scotland and find myself in the middle of a downpour? If I am an honest man, I have to reevaluate my belief system, realizing that it cannot hold up when universally applied.

Any truth, if it is really true, must be universal. It must hold up under *all* circumstances and conditions. If it breaks down, it cannot be called a truth.

Both Lewis and Schaeffer argued with insight and power that when you follow various philosophical explanations of the universe out to the logical conclusions inherent in their presuppositions, the Christian faith is the *only* one truly consistent with the nature of man and the universe as they actually exist. Only Christianity holds up all the way. Only Christianity is capable of answering *all* the circumstances and conditions of the universe and the human condition. Every other worldview breaks down eventually.

Now a man may devise his own private little Sahara, and come up with a worldview that explains everything to his satisfaction. But somewhere else on the planet it is going to rain, and where is his worldview then?

Consistency. That is the key.

Does belief answer the criterion of life and the world? And can you *live* on the basis of what you say you believe—no matter where you take those beliefs?

The inconsistent cannot be true. A philosophical position that cannot hold up and be lived out at the logical extension of its fundamental suppositions—such is a philosophical position that cannot be true.

Schaeffer and Lewis exercised profound impact on both the believing and the unbelieving world. Non-Christians flocked to hear Schaeffer. Lewis was on the cover of *Time* magazine. The world listened because, despite the inconsistency of many of the positions they hold, people generally place a value on common sense and reasonable thinking.

Both men were admired even by those who disagreed with them, because they could see that the minds of these two Christian thinkers were keen, and that they were honest and sincere in their desire to find and communicate truth.

I find it curious and disturbing, however, to realize how little Christians have sought to move to finality *inside* the doctrines of faith.

We admire it outside the wall, where the intellectual battle is waged with the unbelieving world by Christian apologists. We enjoy watching men like Lewis take a Sahara-desert-philosopher to the middle of a rain forest and douse the irrationality of his worldview. We relish seeing non-Christians put in their place, as it were, for the illogic between supposition and conclusion.

But we are loath to look at such holes *within our own thought systems*. We have not trained ourselves to think with logic, reason, insight, and common sense about many of the doctrines we hold as part of our belief. Our reluctance to accept the totality of God's goodness is but one example.

Following suppositions out to the logical extensions of our assumptions is an exercise many are utterly unacquainted with. The whole concept is probably unknown to half of those reading this book.

Here is the point I would make: It is important to follow things to the end *inside* the Christian faith as well as *outside* it. To be effective and consistent believers, Christians need to

> IT IS IMPORTANT TO FOLLOW THINGS TO THE END *INSIDE* THE CHRISTIAN FAITH AS WELL AS *OUTSIDE* IT.

look at their viewpoints, and follow them all the way to their logical conclusions. We've got to see if what we believe makes sense, and even more importantly, whether we can live consistently on the basis of what we say we believe.

Do our beliefs hold up? Can our beliefs be consistently lived by?

Not enough Christians have been asking these questions, inquiring whether the tenets we have long assumed true can, in fact, be supported out at their end points.

It is fearfully easy to live *inconsistently* with the precepts of our faith, dwelling in the valley, refusing to venture, because of the rigors of the climb, to the mountains of bold faith.

That is why it has taken so long for us to get to this point in our journey. Now, however, we have reached the point at which we must break open our previously limited understanding so that we may move to the heights of God's Fatherhood.

How do we get inside the husks...how do we live by the truths we discover...how do we scale at last the highest pinnacles of faith?

By following the principles and attributes of God's Fatherhood to finality, by extending the suppositions that we say we believe all the way out to their logical conclusions.

This statement is anything but merely intellectual. It is one of the most practical things any of us will ever do.

O God, help our faith to be real and true and consistent...all the way to the farthest end points of what we say we believe!

29

DO WE REALLY BELIEVE IN GOD'S FATHERHOOD?

AFTER ALL THIS TIME IT MAY SEEM LUDICROUS TO YOU that I would ask such a question, "Do we believe in God's Fatherhood?"

But the question is: "Do we *really* believe in God's Fatherhood?"

We've got to find out.

To grasp God's Fatherhood in a dynamic way that will change a former "acquaintance" with Him into a *knowing* of intimacy, we first have to discover whether we really believe what we say about Him.

Most of what we might call the "attributes" of God's Fatherhood are familiar to most of us. Given 60 seconds, we could each list 15 or 20. We possess a ready-made informational composite we could recite as quickly as the multiplication table.

We know these things because they have been emphasized in our Sunday school classes and Bible studies, and we've heard them from the pulpit.

But do we know how to live *in* the reality of that Fatherhood?

It is infinitely better to apprehend *one* truth of God's

> IT IS INFINITELY BETTER TO APPREHEND ONE TRUTH OF GOD'S BEING THAN TO KNOW TEN THOUSAND FACTS ABOUT GOD.

being—a *full* truth, a "live" truth—and apprehend it to its core, and then live in the reality of that discovery, than to know ten thousand facts about God and not live in them.

In the spiritual realm, gathering intellectual information is a pointless exercise. If this inner journey means anything for you, I pray it means you have been helped to *live* in what you know, whether that be one truth, or the entire scope of Fatherhood.

It is a process of discovery no one can carry out for you. It is personal and internal.

Even Jesus had to go through it. What was He doing in the Temple at age 12? He had embarked on the quest to know His Father.

How did He spend the years between 12 and 30? Sometime during that period His earthly father, Joseph, died. There was clearly great love between them. Can you not imagine Jesus wrestling through His relationship with His Father in Heaven alongside His life with Joseph?

Jesus didn't merely float onto the scene in the first chapter of Mark out of a 30-year vacuum. He was a living, breathing, thinking, feeling human being. What did His temptation in the wilderness entail? Jesus was probing the limits of His Father's goodness and trustworthiness.

He had to *know* His Father. Anything less than *full* conviction that His Father was good and could be utterly trusted, and Jesus might have turned back and returned to the safety of Galilee when the moment of ultimate trial came in Gethsemane.

He had to go through the process of discovery and then take that personal, intimate *knowing* of the Father and *live* by it—and die by it—all the way to the end...to finality.

Jesus had to travel the uncertain paths to the mountaintops of Fatherhood too.

He is our example.

Jesus followed every one of the attributes of His Father to finality: at age 12, in His youth, after Joseph died, as He worked in the carpenter's shop providing for His family, in the desert battling satan, in the garden, on the cross, in the tomb, in the very depths of hell itself, and on the first Easter morning.

He *knew* His Father!

That's how I want to know the Father of Jesus too. It is to such a quest that I have dedicated my life. When I read those magnificent words in John 17:20-26, I find myself swallowed up and taken *inside* that prayer. It moves me beyond description. As George MacDonald said, "I am lost in the wonder of the thing."[1]

Jesus prayed...for *me*! Can you imagine!

He prayed that I would know His Father!

I hunger with a longing I cannot describe to yield myself so fully to the purposes of God that He can indeed fulfill Jesus' words in my life.

Oh, to be part of the answer to that mighty pouring out of love from the Son to the Father!

ENDNOTE

1. George MacDonald, *Unspoken Sermons*, Third Series (Eureka, CA: Sunrise Books, 1996), p. 19.

30

DISCOVERING WHETHER GOD IS REALLY GOOD

LOOK UP, MY FELLOW TRAVELERS, AND BEHOLD a great yet astonishingly simple truth—God the Father is *good*!

Astonishing, you say. How so? It is an elementary theological principle.

Indeed, a theological "principle" according to valley theologies, that then proceed to explain away its import.

But here it is no mere doctrinal *principle*, but a live *truth*. It is goodness that is beginning to enable us to see with new clarity. For goodness is the very oxygen of the high mountains where God dwells!

Most believers would say, "Of course God is good."

When adversity comes, however, what do we do? Ordinarily we do not rejoice. When suffering comes, we grumble and grouse and complain.

If we truly believe the Father is good, and believe that He is always doing His very best for His creatures, and if His goodness is truly one of the central truths of our being, then we will *know* all is well—in the midst of any and all adversity.

We will rejoice.

The Father's goodness will be a truth we live in all the way, *out to the end* even in the midst of suffering. When circumstances appear "bad," we know otherwise. All the way to finality. When the rains come, they do not cause us to lose heart because our belief system is consistent no matter what.

Suffering, crisis, heartache, natural disaster, even death abound in this world. Yet there resides in the depths of our soul a calm serenity and quietude. We know that God is still good—all the way to the end, to finality...absolutely...utterly.

For the mature Christian, some of this outlook is hinted at. Yes, there exists a peace, even in dark circumstance. Yet when faced with the horrible, cruel, unjust suffering we witness around us, would we not admit to places deep inside where we find ourselves "wondering" about the totality of God's goodness? Perhaps such occasional doubts expose our seeming "peace" as something more like resignation rather than an energetic, living trust.

When I see the world's heartbreaking grief, the starving and dying all over our planet, the homeless, innocent victims of crime, the modern scourge of abortion, the seeming injustice of circumstance, the devastation of war, I *have* wondered how far God's goodness goes.

Yes...I wrestle through the question of how far God's goodness extends. I struggled with it just weeks ago, after this book was already completed and into the production process, when we received a phone call from a dear young lady who had been living with us and had gone home for Christmas.

"My brother was killed last night," she said.

As long as I have been walking with the Lord, I suddenly found myself face-to-face with the most fundamental issue of all—the extent of God's love. How could I, one who believed in the limitlessness of God's love and goodness, frame a meaningful response to our friends, the young man's stunned parents and brothers and sisters?

The first thing that always comes to mind is, "Why did God let this happen?"

But God does not necessarily always *let* or *not let* such things happen. Things...just happen. God does not *cause* pain and suffering. They are simply part of the equation of life. His sovereignty and goodness exist on a higher plane, giving meaning and comfort even in the midst of events that He will not control. But through such events—the good and the bad—His love and goodness, rather than His control of life's details, remain sovereign.

Where is the end point, the limit, to God's goodness? Is it really... could it *possibly*...truly be...*infinite*?

What do I say to the woman whose letter I read just yesterday, who said, "I know we were not promised fairness, but sometimes it just seems like God went on sabbatical and put out His 'Do Not Disturb' sign. He seems so far away and so unreachable. I have a difficult time trying to understand why He bothered to allow me to live."

What do my wife and I say to ourselves when the private grief we share alone becomes insurmountable?

Do I have easy answers...for our friends who lost a son, for hurting people who write us...or for ourselves?

Life is hard. Life contains pain.

It *is* difficult to follow a *good* Fatherhood all the way to finality. I'm not going to try to pretend it's easy. At some point, for every one of us, that goodness threatens to break down. The rain begins to fall. We find our belief system facing the ultimate test.

I've succumbed, as I'm sure all of you have, to the persistent human tendency to reduce God's goodness to the finite regions where my mind can figure it out, where I can box it up and define it, explain it, or try to understand it.

How else do we deal with the seeming cruelty and arbitrary inconsistency of the Old Testament and the pain and suffering that exist in the world? How else do we try to cope with heartbreak in our own families? The struggle between humanity and eternity is *real*...painful...confusing.

It's a conundrum of epic proportions.

We all engage in this intellectual tug-of-war at the foundation point of belief, or we glibly retreat into the intellectual dishonesty of saying, "Well, that's God's will...it's not for me to understand."

If we're capable of serious thought, and if we're honest with ourselves, we *do* limit God to our finite capacity to understand.

The instant we do, however, we lessen our capacity to truly *know* Him...as He is. We shrink Him to fit *our* mentality, rather than stretching ourselves past the husk, past the shell, into the high reaches of His infinite being and character.

So what is the answer? It is not an *easy* one. But it is an answer that resounds with truth.

God is good. And all will come right in the end. It may not come right tomorrow...but it will come right in the end.

Somehow we must cling to that truth, and learn to make it real. It is not easy. It is not easy for me. But I know truth is there that I must not let go of.

> GOD IS GOOD. AND ALL WILL COME RIGHT IN THE END. IT MAY NOT COME RIGHT TOMORROW...BUT IT WILL COME RIGHT IN THE END.

One of the key steps, therefore, in the process of discovering how to live in God's Fatherhood does not involve memorizing a list of traits, but discovering what those attributes really *mean* when followed to the end.

My telling you "God is good," however, won't enable you to know and live in the truths of Fatherhood.

Goodness at that point is just a mere word representing the shell around an attribute most of us would have to admit we still do not grasp very clearly where suffering and cruelty slam against it.

There are all sorts of theological shadow dances around such difficulties. But many of them make as much sense as the emperor's invisible robes, and with similar result. We delude no one but ourselves with theologic double-talk. The world is not fooled...which is one reason for the most part it's not paying much attention.

To live in God's goodness requires the following of that *goodness* to finality. Do you *really* believe the Father is good—in your brain, in your heart, in all your thoughts and attitudes and beliefs and relationships and decisions, in how you view Scripture, in how you respond to the world...in everything?

Now we're beginning to scale the high mountains of faith where intimacy begins to reward those who diligently seek Him.

When we live and believe what we *say* we believe, indeed will the world take notice.

This profound truth was revealed to me nearly 30 years ago, when a friend who had just returned from Schaeffer's L'Abri in Switzerland was visiting with my wife and me.

A calm was evident in his carriage, a new maturity. Judy asked him, "If you had to boil it down to one thing you learned from your time at L'Abri, what would it be?"

Our friend was quiet. Very thoughtful. The air hung heavy in our living room with silent expectation. It was obviously a huge, encompassing question for him.

When he finally spoke, his voice was quiet, but so earnest, with a quality of solidity and tenderness and love. His words carried a Rock of Gibraltar strength.

"That God is good," he replied.

None of the three of us said anything for a long time. We merely sat soaking in the depth and implication of his answer.

That single word *good* rang with such quiet force and power that I have never forgotten the moment.

Those four words have been with Judy and me ever since.

Our friend had been a Christian for years—a solid, growing Christian. He had spent the past months studying, learning, reading. He had probably learned 50 new things about his Christian faith.

But it all reduced down to one single element of God's Fatherhood which he no longer knew merely intellectually. He had gotten hold of it at a profoundly more personal level, and it had changed him.

The "principle" had become a *live truth*. He had gazed more deeply into the thing called God's "goodness," and had found out something more about the life that was contained inside.

At L'Abri the shell broke wide open, and life came pouring out.

31

THE FOUR MOUNTAIN PEAKS OF FATHERHOOD

OUR JOURNEY THUS FAR TOGETHER has been largely preparational, even devotional, rather than informational.

We have been getting ourselves ready, not so much turning over new ground as spading the hard soil of existing beliefs so that it will be capable of growing those plants and bearing that fruit intended to blossom in our hearts.

We have been preparing our eyes to see in new ways, enabling us to look more deeply into truths we have known all along.

Climbing past these initial plateaus has been necessary because they have led us ever upward, following the footsteps of Jesus toward the heights at which we now find ourselves, where so much more is visible.

As we cast our gaze upward from this new vantage point, we behold four great mountain peaks. These are the heights toward which we have been journeying. They represent the high summits of the Father's being. We are now prepared to see them in all their glory.

The first is the tallest, the others stand slightly lower and around its sides. These are truths whose foothills we have long been familiar with:

God the Father is *love*.

God the Father is *good*.

God the Father is *trustworthy.*

God the Father is *forgiving.*

Many lesser peaks dot the horizon of our view in many directions, but these tower above the rest.

GOD THE FATHER IS *LOVE, GOOD, TRUSTWORTHY,* AND *FORGIVING.*

And there, nestled at the point where these four peaks converge, lies the mansion of the Father's estate! From its innermost chamber flow forth the waters of life.

It is here He desires us to make our home. God wants His people to take the four powerful truths into their innermost being. He wants us to live in those resounding truths every moment.

Do we dare move closer? Do we trust Jesus' word that His Father is indeed completely and *infinitely* good, that He will *always* forgive, that we may trust Him for *all* things, and that there is nothing whatever we need fear from Him?

> *Strengthen our hearts, Father of Jesus. We desire to press forward. But the air is so new to breathe. Help us, we pray! Lead us to the center of Your home where You would have Your family dwell with You.*

32

THE HEART
CHAMBER OF LIFE

TENTATIVELY, AS JESUS LEADS, WE VENTURE TOWARD the magnificent mansion of the Father's home.

Through the door and into the inner chamber He guides us.

There we find the Father Himself awaiting our arrival!

One look in His smiling face tells us He is not the Fearsome Sovereign we thought no man could look upon lest he die. He is just as Jesus has told us. He is the Father of the prodigal—watching and waiting, arms outstretched. His face is full of love.

Jesus bids us continue.

Speechless we approach the Father's presence, unable still, after all Jesus has said, to keep from timidity, though the expression of love on His face dissipates the last lingering shadows of valley fear.

Both the Father and Jesus are smiling broadly, unreserved in their joy to bring us here to share their divine familyhood.

We know now that this is where we belong!

This is the home for which we have hungered all our life! The quest of our heart, our mind, our soul, our will has reached its culmination, its final destination!

Jesus takes us straight to the Father, then places our tiny hand in His.

Henceforth, Jesus says, *just as I instructed My disciples to do, you are to call Him Abba...Daddy...Father!*

Now at last the Father Himself speaks.

His voice is not what we had expected. It is neither

> ## JESUS SAYS, *JUST AS I INSTRUCTED MY DISCIPLES TO DO, YOU ARE TO CALL HIM ABBA...DADDY...FATHER!*

thunderous nor loud, neither stern nor reproving. It is the tenderest, kindest, most soothing and Fatherly voice we could imagine. It is strong and resonant, but with invitation not reproach. The very sound, as the words fall from His lips, makes us want to run into His arms and jump into the lap of His embrace.

You may make your home here, the Father says, *in these innermost rooms of My presence. Here...with Me. It is your choice, of course. Many of My sons and daughters do not so choose, but I hope you will. That is why I sent My Son to the valley to bring you here to Me. Come!*

Still holding our hand, the Father now leads us farther inside. We find ourselves entering a huge room more magnificent than imagination can describe. Though we thought we had seen the extent of the mansion as we approached from the outside, now we see how mistaken we were. For in all directions we behold no wall of boundary anywhere. The inside of the palace goes on without end. The inside is larger than the outside.

Knowing our thoughts, the Father speaks:

This is the chamber where My love, goodness, trustworthiness, and forgiveness dwell. And you are correct, there are no walls herein, for My love and goodness and forgiveness extend forever. This is the mansion of My presence, the heart of My being. This is where I invite all My sons and daughters to dwell.

As He says the words, for the first time the smile leaves the Father's face, but only for a moment. Then He says, *Come in still further. I have more to show you.*

120

He leads toward a great fountain where mighty waters spring up thundering from deep within the earth. A massive emerald pool of unfathomable depth extends around the spring, out of which emanate innumerable streams and rivers and brooks of varying size and swiftness, flowing off in a hundred directions.

Again the Father speaks.

The waters of My life flow out from here, from My heart of love, to all the earth.

"Even to the valley?" we ask.

Yes, no one in the valley could live an instant without the nourishment of these waters, though they know it not, nor do they have the faintest inclination where they originate.

"But they talk about You...so differently than all this. It sometimes seems they don't know of the four peaks. Why don't You tell them how You really are?"

Ah, My child, answers the Father, *I am constantly telling them, in a thousand ways. My Son has told them. My servants through the ages have told them. Everything I have made tells them—shouts to them—of these waters and these high mountains where I beckon them...Look! Then come! These waters give life to the whole earth, and I have placed hints of these waters, reminders of the home of this chamber, small sounds of My voice, into everything I have made. I am constantly encouraging them to **see** and **hear** in a thousand ways. But alas, it is wearying work for My Son and My Spirit to open their eyes and unplug their ears.*

"I am thankful You were so patient with me," we find ourselves saying, "and that You brought me here."

I desire that you make your dwelling with Me, the Father says, *smiling broadly. Come...drink of the waters of My divine self. For this you came... now drink.*

We stoop down and set our lips to the green pool of life.

The water is like nothing we have ever tasted!

With the first sip, suddenly we feel the refreshing springs of living water filling to overflowing every once-thirsty reservoir within us.

The water you are drinking is the water of My love, which is the essence of My being, the Father says. *Only the waters from this spring satisfy all thirsts, in all hearts, removing all cares, bringing peace in all things. Henceforth, this is to be the divine well of your sustenance.*

33

LIVING IN THE FOURFOLD
HEART OF GOD'S PRESENCE

WHAT WE HAVE JUST HEARD FROM THE FATHER HIMSELF is so vastly different from what we had learned about Him in the valley assemblies where a different path toward spirituality was taught.

Here, the Father continues, *is to be your home. I have prepared this just for you, and for all the offspring of My heart. My family dwells here—My Son, My Spirit, My children, as well as Myself. Here—in My love, My goodness, My trustworthiness, and My forgiveness. This is the source of life, even My own divine life. This is where My I-am-ness originates...and here will you be with Me forever. My nature is not waiting to chastise, to punish, nor to exact retribution. Rather I am eager to forgive and shower My love upon creation.*

Make yourself at home here...in My heart of love. Not only do I love the world, I love ***you***. *I will accomplish only good. You may trust Me.*

The most basic truth in all the universe, lying open in the pages of Scripture for all to see, the foundation for the Kingdom of God itself and for *all* existence throughout creation, is nothing more nor less than this: God really is just what the Bible says of Him—He is *love*.

In only one passage throughout God's Word does a biblical writer take it upon himself actually to define God's being. You know where it is. The writer was the disciple whom Jesus loved.

Who is God? What is He like? What are the attributes of His vast personality and character? What is the summation of His being?

> **GOD REALLY IS JUST WHAT THE BIBLE SAYS OF HIM—HE IS *LOVE*.**

John told us near the end of his first letter: *God is love.*

Many lesser aspects combine to make up the full multifaceted breadth of His character. But they are all subservient to that great high-mountain, defining truth that what He *is*, is love!

This is the highest summit of His being.

Just behind it, and only slightly lower, stand the truths of goodness, trustworthiness, and forgiveness so intrinsic to love.

All other attributes of His infinite being—thousands of them!—are swallowed up within the magnitude of these four.

These are the guiding principles of Genesis 2 life with the Father, toward which Jesus came to earth to lead us. It is these four we are to live in as we walk the high mountain regions with our Father.

These truths, because they comprise the Father's heart, are to be our home. Such was God's plan from the beginning.

Are they just too good to be true?

They are just so good they must be true!

> *Father, forgive us our unbelieving and untrusting heart! Why can we not bring ourselves to believe that You, our Father, really are good?*
>
> *Oh, but if You are God, if You are love, then how could You be other than good?*

Why is it so difficult for us to trust You to be absolutely loving and good and forgiving...all the way to the most difficult places...all the way into the most hidden corners of our own self?

Throw aside the coverings, throw wide the cellar doors of our being! Invade every inch, illuminate us everywhere with the probing light of Your truth-searching Spirit.

Fill the reservoirs and cisterns within us with the waters of Your precious self! It is to know You that we have undertaken this journey. Fill us, we pray, to overflowing...only with You!

Help us, O God, our good, loving, trustworthy, forgiving Father. Reveal yet more of Your being to us.

Now that we have arrived in the mountains where the waters of Your life gush forth to fill us and where You Yourself live, help us now, more than ever, to call You Father!

34

A CONVERSATION
WITH THE SON

At FIRST WE RELISH LIFE WITHIN THE FATHER'S LOVE, GOODNESS, trustworthiness, and forgiveness with all the abandonment of the Abba-delighted child.

Our first days are full of great joy, as if an unseen weight has been lifted from our shoulders whenever we think of the Father. But then gradually new questions begin to present themselves.

Reminders of other aspects of God's nature begin to plague us with discomforting questions...about His holiness, about the eternal consequences of sin, about that darker side of His being which we had formerly been taught was so different than that represented by the high peak of infinite forgiveness.

As from out of the distance, precepts and teachings from the valley, deeply ingrained from past ways of thinking, intrude. They remind us that the Father's estate is much larger than we can see from here. Then we begin to notice a great many others about, moving to and fro carrying containers of great variety.

Where do all these people live? we wonder. What is it they are about?

Our elder Brother has already noticed our concern. One morning, therefore, He bids us rise early and accompany Him to the distant regions of this land. Along the way He tells us what we are going to see.

Our Father's estate, He says, *is of far vaster extent than many imagine. Its reaches are immense—limitless by measurement known to mortal man.*

"Is there no end to it?" we ask.

> ## OUR FATHER'S ESTATE IS OF FAR VASTER EXTENT THAN MANY IMAGINE.

It is said there is, Jesus replies with a smile.

"What about the limitations of man's devising?" we wonder, remembering the disquiet we have been feeling for several days.

Again comes a smile to Jesus' face, although one tinged with sadness.

There are many such limitations, He says slowly, *and they grieve our Father. But as you say, they are not the Father's. Because the fog of their theologic brains obscures the tops of the four peaks, many assume that the mountains of goodness and forgiveness extend no higher than their short-sighted vision can see.*

"Why doesn't the Father blow away the fog from their minds?"

*Some fogs He can do nothing to break up. They are too thick. These dear ones have free will. If such people insist on seeing these mountains as only tiny hills, He can do nothing until they **want** to perceive the infinitely more that is in His heart to accomplish.*

"And if they never come to want that more?"

Then they will have to wait until death helps them see how wrong their fogbound theologies were. How much better for the Father's people to discover the infinite reach of His love during their earthly life. But that their explanations so limit the ultimate reach of His reconciliatory purpose will not keep all that is in the Father's heart from being accomplished.

"Does the Father make no limits then," we ask, "draw no ultimate lines, fix no end points?"

Oh yes. There are borders to His land, Jesus replies.

"Where then?"

They are not meant for mortals to see. He pauses, as if remembering fondly a conversation with a friend.

When the Father does draw lines of dividing, He continues after a moment, *they are pure lines, without breadth, and thus invisible to mortal eyes.*[1] *So you see, the Father's lines cannot be known by man, and so they who make such an attempt their business are bound to err.*

ENDNOTE

1. This concept of *invisible, pure lines without breadth* is taken from George Mac-Donald's *David Elginbrod* (Eureka, CA: Sunrise Books, 1999), p. 372.

35

BORDERLANDS SHORT
OF ULTIMATE FATHERHOOD

WE WALK ON WITH JESUS IN SILENCE a good while.

Suddenly we realize that we have come a great distance from the Father's mountain mansion. The terrain has changed. The greenery here is not nearly so lush. The high waters are already thinning. Less of their emerald color sparkles now in the grasses and leaves.

Nor are we walking alone. The way is actually growing crowded, with considerably more bustle and activity than higher up. We are greeted as we pass. Everyone knows Jesus and speaks familiarly with Him. Once again we notice the containers they are carrying.

Suddenly with alarm we realize the air is changing too. The crisp atmosphere of the high region has begun to give way to the old familiar feel of the valley fog.

Then we realize that we have been descending all morning.

"Where are we going?" we ask in anxiety. "Are You taking me back to the valley?"

Have no fear, Jesus reassures us. *There were many questions on your mind earlier. We are going to visit some of the low-lying borderlands where you will find answers to them.*

"Did you not say that the borders of the estate were far away?"

They are. These are not "borderlands" because they are near the boundaries, only because they are far down the slopes from My Father's home. They are the frontier outposts, lying in the fringe regions, but we are still within the precincts of the Father's land.

"Who are all these people?"

Your brothers and sisters, My Father's own sons and daughters.

"They are part of His family?"

Yes, certainly.

"Then why do they live so far out here, so far down in the lowlands?"

They choose to.

"But why? It is not nearly so pleasant. The air is not at all so invigorating. The water here does not tingle with such vibrancy of life."

All you say is correct, and it is a puzzle. But they are more comfortable here.

We cannot imagine it. Especially since they seem familiar with the mountain places.

Why do you say that? asks Jesus, responding to our thought.

"Because they are walking up and down. Were not many of them up there earlier?"

They sojourn there, it is true, He nods. *But they do not have eyes to see the Father's home for what it is. They merely conduct their business and then return. Their lungs are not accustomed to the high air.*

"By their business, do You mean those containers they are carrying?"

Yes.

"What are they?"

They are for gathering water from the wells and pools outside the mansion, where accumulates some of the overflow from our Father's springs. They bring it back down here to where they live.

"But I understood there was room enough for all the Father's family up there."

There is. Vastly more than sufficient room for all who would dwell there.

"Why don't they then?"

They would rather cart the meager containers of the Father's life down the hill, and come back for more when then need it, than live where they can fill themselves with His Being constantly from the source. They only sip at the Father's goodness. They are afraid to drink of it to the fill. They are afraid too much goodness will lessen His divine holiness. They dabble out His forgiveness with sprinkles from reluctant fingers, as if the world is experiencing a draught from the waters of life. It grieves our Father. But such is their choice. Until they choose otherwise, there is little anyone can do to dissuade them from their scanty belief in His goodness.

> *THEY ARE AFRAID TOO MUCH GOODNESS WILL LESSEN HIS DIVINE HOLINESS. THEY DABBLE OUT HIS FORGIVENESS WITH SPRINKLES FROM RELUCTANT FINGERS, AS IF THE WORLD IS EXPERIENCING A DRAUGHT FROM THE WATERS OF LIFE*

"But can't they be told? Surely if they only knew what it was like inside the great mansion...surely if they knew of the emerald pool, they would..."

They have been told...in a thousand ways. All have been told. You should understand. You were once of their number too. You lived many years in the valley. Telling is not required...but hearing.

"But this is not the valley. I thought we were within the Father's estate?"

We are. But you will find many pockets of valley dwellers in our Father's family. Of the places I will show you, some are higher on the slopes than others. Some, sad to say, live so low as to be quite suffocated by valley fogs. Those who make their homes in such parched regions find the high air so difficult to breathe that they must make quick work of it when they venture up to gather the water they need.

"That is beyond belief. The air up there is easier to breathe!"

Not for them. They have so accustomed themselves to the fictional fabrications of their theologies, calling our Father by so many names of their own devising, inventing so many illogical necessities, as they call them, that stem from their distorted views of His character, that when they get too close to the reality of His presence of love and forgiveness, they find themselves suffocating in their own inconsistency. They are more comfortable with doctrines about Him, than with the reality of His goodness. Maintaining their theologies is more important to them than the Father Himself.

"But why? I cannot understand it!"

A few taste the high air and instantly all thought of doctrinal fog becomes loathsome. But many others find it just the opposite. They cannot stand the sting of accountability the high air causes. Their comfort is found in the traditions of their valley elders, and their valley explanations of God's ways.

We walk on, reflecting on all He has said.

Looking up after some time, we find ourselves approaching what appears to be a heavily inhabited settlement. As we come near, everyone greets Jesus with relieved and appreciative smiles.

They seem on the most intimate of terms with Him, though we cannot help but notice the anxious looks they continually cast up the mountain in the direction from which we have come.

We look about, then at last see a small signpost at the entry to the place. It reads: *City of Fear.*

36

Low-lying Communities

THE FATHER'S KINGDOM INCLUDES many low-lying border regions where His people make their homes rather than dwell in the high country.

All are invited to live in that home prepared for the Father's family where it is located in the highest regions surrounded by Love, Goodness, Trustworthiness, and Forgiveness.

However, many choose instead to live elsewhere. They feel more comfortable in the cities of fear, justice, denominationalism, grace, atonement, or in the villages of justification, predestination, evangelicalism, omnipotence, sanctification, omnipresence, wrath, spiritual gifts, or endtimes.

> ALL ARE INVITED TO LIVE IN THAT HOME SURROUND-ED BY LOVE, GOODNESS, TRUSTWORTHINESS, AND FORGIVENESS.

We have seen that *fear*, properly understood according to the Father-child relationship of Genesis 2, is the beginning of a proper relationship of *childness* toward our Father.

But are we to *live* in that part of His Kingdom where fear rules?

As a place from which to start our upward journey, fear points an accurate direction. But is the City of Fear a place for the development of a complete spiritual perspective? A thousand times no!

Fear is a mere beginning point.

What about the village of *omnipotence*? Is it a place flowing with milk and honey?

God is omnipotent without question. But scratching out an existence while attempting to live only in that desolate corner of His Kingdom is difficult indeed.

Oh, friends, why do our dear brothers and sisters want to live where provision is so scant? So little food is to be found in the environs of the village of omnipotence. A kind of living starvation often results for those intent to remain there. No one there has the faintest idea what *Abba* means.

Nearby sits another village called *omnipresence*. Is it a portion of the Kingdom where comfortable dwellings can be built?

More to sustain life tends to grow there. On the whole its residents are much healthier than the citizens of omnipotence. Yet the place still makes for an incomplete and superficial sort of life.

Is *justice* part of God's being? Of course, the Bible tells us so.

But He does not want us making our home in His justice, though many Christians do.

Oh, but I feel bad for the residents of justice. It must be such a somber and chilly place!

The ground there is hard, and the only food it is able to produce contains a certain sourness that takes away a good deal of the pleasure of eating.

The elevation is low, too, affecting the quality of air, and making the place far more susceptible to the infiltration of valley fogs than is altogether healthy.

As far away from the living center as it is, however, many of the Father's sons and daughters choose to construct their homes in the city of justice. Land there is inexpensive and building materials, though not of the highest quality, are readily available even to the most unskilled of carpenters. It is one of the ancient cities of the Kingdom as well, with a long history that its residents feel qualifies it as perhaps the most important city of the land.

It lies far down the slopes, well away from the heart of the estate. Jesus visits from time to time, and they are always glad to see Him, reminding themselves that He was "the necessary satisfaction for God's justice."

Is *wrath* an aspect of God's nature? Of course, the Bible tells us so.

But He does not want us making our home in the village of wrath, though sadly many try to erect a chilly domicile there.

Wrath is found upon the grounds of the Father's estate, and we do well to know its location and the causes for its incitement. But it lies at the bottommost point of all, on the very valley floor. It is continually covered by the valley fog, and the high mountains of Fatherhood are nearly entirely cut off from view.

Those in residence in that bleak, gray region still suffer from the illusion that the Master of the estate is an ogre whom they must not approach too closely.

When Jesus visits, they sigh with relief, discussing ever and again their gratefulness for His "taking God's wrath on Himself." They never see the tears in Jesus' eyes that they so misunderstand His relationship with the Father.

It must pull at the Father's heart to see them working so much harder than necessary to eke out an existence in those frigid and airless wastes, barely surviving when He has so much life to give them higher up.

Is God's being full of *grace*? Of course, the Bible tells us so.

But He does not want us making our *home* in His grace either.

Grace lies on the other side of the estate, several days' journey from wrath and justice. In fact, it is such a warm and cheerful and altogether happy place that a great multitude have built homes there and are quite comfortable. It is one of the largest cities within the Father's Kingdom with a temperate, year-round climate.

The ground there is soft and grows a number of things of itself without the need of much tilling. The city of grace sits higher on the slopes than many lesser villages, and more of the waters from above trickle down, though its green is paler than emerald. In the land of grace, the peak of forgiveness is visible, and this attribute of the Father's heart is understood more clearly than lower in the valley.

But so little of the hard and vigorous work of the estate gets accomplished there. Seventh-day leisure is the predominant element of its spiritual creed. In truth, the city is in large measure a recreation and retirement community for many citizens of the Kingdom.

Alas, not many laborers and warriors come from the land of grace, for the food and air there do not produce stalwart and vigorous constitutions.

There are expeditions to be mounted, both higher up into the distant hills out of sight, and back into the valley. There are fences to tend, battles with the great enemy to wage...so much to be done. The Father needs stouthearted and manly sons and daughters to be about His tasks.

Is *holiness* part of God's being? Most assuredly.

But He does not even want us making our home in His holiness.

Holiness is found on slopes of exceeding height on the distant borders of the estate. There is no village, no community of holiness, only a snow-capped peak by that name, so high it is invisible through the clouds that constantly surround it.

Many of the Father's own do live there, but they cannot scale that peak until the time for such ascension is ordained by the Father and He takes them there Himself. There is no oxygen there for us at present. It is impossible for our kind to survive there. We cannot breathe the rarified air. Those regions require new lungs to grasp how infinite holiness coexists with infinite forgiveness. It is air not intended for mortals to breathe.

Occasional visionaries attempt to scale the sheer face of righteousness leading to Mount Holiness, but always with the same result. Those who insist upon trying are either injured in the attempt and eventually return to live out the remainder of their days in the valley. Or else they tumble down time and again, back to the region of grace.

Certainly the Father will take us to gaze up the mountains of righteousness and holiness from time to time. He says that someday we shall receive new lungs and then we shall be capable of dwelling there.

When we live in the Father's love, goodness, trustworthiness, and forgiveness, He makes use of all the other attributes of His infinitely complex nature—according to their perfect and infinite, not partial and finite purposes. Then will He reveal His *whole* Self and thus transform us steadily by degrees into sons and daughters who bear the stamp and image of His own personality and character.

As we gaze about, we see many such communities of like-mindedness where God's people dwell comfortably together, rarely mounting expeditions higher up toward the presence of His Fatherhood.

We see cities with denominational labels. We see the huge metropolitan regions of Anglicanism and Catholicism and Orthodoxy, each with millions of inhabitants. We see the city of evangelicalism, with its suburbs of worship and praise and music and prophecy and spiritual gifts and ministry. We see other villages and cities and communities with many diverse names and labels over their gates, reflecting their founders, their chief doctrines, the emphasis of their historical movements, their hallowed days of worship. Most are enclosed about with high walls of exclusion, to all appearances intended to keep out all except those of like doctrinal persuasion.

But then a shocking thought occurs to us. Perhaps the walls have become so high to keep people *in*…intended to *prevent* exploration on the high slopes rising away from the foothills.

For as we gaze out over the expanse of this low-lying landscape, there are so few leaving their assemblies and walled enclosures with eyes wide, looking up toward the mountains, then setting out to discover if somewhere there exists cleaner air to breathe and purer water to drink.

We steal a glance at Jesus beside us. We see tears falling from His eyes. We are reminded of His prayer for the ancient city of Jerusalem, and we

139

know His heart is breaking that so few of these who call themselves His followers are eager to know His Father.

37

B UT W HAT A BOUT...?

C LIMBING BACK TOWARD THE A BBA -MANSION OF OUR NEW HOME at day's end, weary from the excursion to the many communities and villages of the lowlands, we find, to our delight, vigor reviving in our limbs.

Those watching from the spiritual abodes in the low-lying borders and far-flung cities—those shivering and unsmiling in wrath and justice, those with wide smiles but atrophied spiritual muscles in grace, and those millions of satisfied citizens within their variously named communities, churches, movements, and denominations—all look upon us with odd expressions, wondering why we are venturing away from those places where they dwell in such comfort and ease.

As we go, the fresh air of the mountains revives our energy. The way grows quieter as we climb. The crowds and bustle and churchy activity recede behind us.

The gentleman Jesus, kind and wise, allows much room for reflection. He knows the discoveries we have made take time to assimilate.

Much have we seen. A great deal occupies our mind and heart. Yet puzzlement remains about what we had thought about earlier before setting out to the borderlands.

"What about punishment of sin?" we suddenly find ourselves asking after a long silence.

The question startles even us. We hadn't realized it was lurking so near the surface.

"If love is the highest, then…?" we try to continue. But our words trail off and the question remains unfinished.

Jesus smiles.

I am not surprised to hear you ask it, He replies.

"Why? I don't understand."

Perhaps the most common reproach leveled by many of the lowlanders against those who make their home in My Father's heart, is that they are putting aside his hatred of sin in order to take up residence in His love. It is a great fallacy of thinking among the fogbound who cannot see the four peaks. They can make out only the foothills. Therefore they are incapable of apprehending the highest mountain truths.

*To answer you: Our Father **must** eradicate sin from the world. His holiness can never tolerate its evil. This necessity is why He sent Me among you, why I went to the cross. He hates sin. If punishment is required to annihilate it from the universe, verily will He send His righteous punishment.*

"From the places we visited, and what You said about His wrath and justice being smaller than His love, and how they were all taken up in the greater characteristics of His nature, does that mean that the punishment of sin is perhaps less severe?"

Where did you hear a falsehood like that? the words fall quickly from Jesus' lips.

"I thought perhaps…"

You thought His love, because it is the loftiest peak, infinitely higher than our Father's justice, would therefore erase the requirement that sin be atoned for?

"There were those in the lowlands, when they found I had made my home in love, and love only, who implied that I believed such things."

They often think it of those who dwell amongst the peaks. One of the trials that must be borne by the heart-dwelling children is that their own family understands their fellowship with the Father so little. Opposition to the discoveries made on the high slopes is to be expected.

"Opposition by my own brothers and sisters?"

Them most of all.

"But why is it so?"

A smiling Father threatens their established theologies. They take a valley gratification in representing every characteristic of My

> ONE OF THE TRIALS THAT MUST BE BORNE BY THE HEART-DWELLING CHILDREN IS THAT THEIR OWN FAMILY UNDERSTANDS THEIR FELLOWSHIP WITH THE FATHER SO LITTLE.

Father's nature as rooted in what they call His holy hatred of sin. His normal posture, to their distorted view, is angry and stern. Their small view of God is so preoccupied with His holiness that His children can find no room in His heart wherein they may dwell, no smiles within His gruff personality with which to light the dark paths of their gray world. Remember, the city of justice is one of the most ancient of the borderlands, with more deeply entrenched traditions and theologies than most.

Those of such unsmiling countenance pay little heed to what I have told them of the nature of their Father. But He loves them dearly, even in their shortsightedness, and is constantly doing all He can to turn their eyes toward His heart of love.

Be not anxious about what they say. Their eyes are unable yet to penetrate above the fogs. Give Me time with them. I visit them often, and am busily engaged in trying to point their gaze upward.

38

THE ANSWER IS TRUST

"WHAT OF THE THINGS THEY SAY?" WE ASK AT LENGTH. "I want to know all truth, not only the loving side."

That is why we will continue to make excursions throughout the Father's estate, so that you will grasp the fullness of His nature, not just portions of it. But you can only understand the wider extent of our Father's purposes if your home is in the chamber of love.

"Is there truth, then, in their theologies?"

Truth exists in all the places we have visited. Incomplete truth, it may be, but truth indeed. You have seen the fire in the Father's eye, have you not?

"Yes, the warmth of love. I noticed it immediately when You took me to Him."

To you, who approached with humility and the heart of a child, the fire that shone from His eyes was love. You have spoken truly. But to those who rebel against Him, who listen to the serpent and his lies, who set their face contrary to the Father's purposes, that fire is a consuming fire indeed. I have not shown you all there is to see.

We knew instantly what He meant, and shuddered. "Do you mean...?"

There is just such a place as the old legends speak of, He replies, *where the fire rages and the worm dieth not. Hell is no myth, my young brother.*

"I knew it was not," we reply. "But after the four peaks, I found myself just a little confused. Is...is it on the estate?"

145

Far over the peaks, many ranges of mountains distant.

"Who...dwells there?"

Those who are sent. Those from the valley who refuse every invitation to My Father's Kingdom.

"Will You show us that place too?"

Ah, little one, not everything is for you to see at present. If I took you there, you could not understand how the fire of love you beheld in our Father's eyes is the same inferno that rages there. All truths cannot be opened while you are yet a mortal.

"A place such as You speak of seems so different from the wonderful mansion where the emerald waters flow."

As different as black is from white, as different as rebellion is from obedience, as different as death is from life. You perceive it correctly. The look of love in His eyes is always the same, but by necessity it must express itself through different manifestations.

"It is so hard to understand."

That is why one of the peaks is Trustworthiness. You were not given the capacity to understand this matter into which you have inquired. You were given the capacity to trust My Father.

We nod.

When the Father speaks sternly, heed His commands. For truly will those who persist in willful and intentional disobedience discover His anger. The Father is full of love. Love is His very essence. But the fire that burns in His eyes contains no flames of mere earthly consequence. For the closer those who, by choice, have made themselves His children draw into those flaming eyes, the more they are consumed by His love. Those who resist their own childness, however, feel the burning of what must seem to them the very opposite of love.

He is no tame God. Our Father's commands must never be disregarded. Permanent rebellion against Him is eternally life threatening. The eternal furnace is the purifying repository of all sin. Do not forget, young one,

THE ANSWER IS TRUST

I have been there. I had to invade the enemy's temporary camp, there to defeat him, and to release the prisoners from his captivity. Make no mistake, eradication of sin and the refiner's fire necessary to carry out that end, is as intrinsic to our Father's design as are the waters of life that flow from the inner chamber of His mountain home. He will purify the sons of Levi and make them like gold and silver, in order to have men who will bring offerings in righteousness.

"But I still don't understand. If love swallows all, how then...?"

Ah, young one. Put away the algebraic formulas of the valley. The equal signs fall differently up here. All the equations are redrawn when you leave the valley. There is no either-or with our Father. All must be accomplished...all must be fulfilled. Sin must be atoned for. My sacrifice must be brought to infinite completion. Love swallows all, but erases nothing. I died for the world. The Father's infinite will shall be accomplished.

> *LOVE SWALLOWS ALL, BUT ERASES NOTHING. I DIED FOR THE WORLD. THE FATHER'S INFINITE WILL SHALL BE ACCOMPLISHED.*

"But I don't see how...?"

Of course. You cannot. Your eyes are only beginning to see.

Words fail us. We realize instantly the incorrect direction of our thoughts in attempting to equate the seeming disparities of the Father's nature according to valley appearances of likeness.

My young brother, place no limits upon the Father's love in any of the multifold directions in which it expresses itself. None of His attributes, none of His divine purposes, will disappear without being fulfilled. The infinitude of our Father's love is no human love. No man or woman loves sufficiently to discern how righteous justice is to be brought to the aid of fulfilling that love. But our Father is subject to no mortal limitations. His love will accomplish all.

147

Jesus sees how full our heart is, trying to take in the enormity of all He has said.

Fret not over the dilemma these things pose to your human mind, my young brother, He adds. *All is well. You may trust our Father! He is trustworthy in all things, in all ways, and for all the men and women of His creation.*

We can say no more, for we are pondering, as did His own mother, all these truths in our heart.

39

A High View...and More Lofty Vistas Ahead

THE TIME HAS COME, DEAR FRIEND AND FAITHFUL COMPANION in this journey, for us to pause a moment and reflect where we have come.

Does our time together seem brief?

In truth, we have travelled a greater distance in our quest than you may realize.

If one's movement is over flat terrain, round and round in circles traversed many times before, how much progress has there been in the end? As is demonstrated week after week in the assemblies of our land, it is possible to walk 20 miles and get no further than a few yards from your own house.

Direction is more pertinent to progress than how large may be the chunks of ground passing beneath your feet. It is important to know where you are bound.

What makes the outlook from the high places of Fatherhood so spectacular is not so much for how far we have come, but for the still higher and more breathtaking views we have begun to catch sight of ahead.

"But our journey together is nearly done," you say. "I am eager to continue, but it is clear you are almost through."

For the present, perhaps. It is true, the time has come for us to part company.

It is necessary that it be so. The Fatherhood of God remains inexhaustible. The discoveries awaiting you as you move toward those still higher and deeper regions of intimacy with Him are discoveries into which He Himself must lead you.

I must continue my own quest with our mutual Father, as He leads me, and allow you to do the same. He will be your guide now.

As you go, remember the principles we have discovered along the paths we have trod together.

Continue to look up. Heed your instinct. It is the whisper of Fatherhood calling, reminding, urging, exhorting, inviting you into the intimacy of His presence.

Look for the Father in the quiet, hidden places. The divine fingerprint exists in all He has touched. His emerald waters imbue the whole universe with life.

Seek not intellectual information. *Pursue instead the Father's character.* He delights to reveal Himself, but such revelation comes only to those who seek Him. Open your eyes to *see.*

Putting fear in its proper perspective, neither reverencing it nor ignoring it, *follow God's Fatherhood to finality* in the four fundamental characteristics of His being. His works are completely and only *good*, you may *trust* Him utterly, His *forgiveness* will be victorious and complete, for what He is, is *love.*

Make your home in the center of His mansion...*in His very heart.* Fill every corner, every cistern within you of the life-giving waters of His Fatherhood.

Travel throughout the entire estate of the Father's Kingdom, learning about all aspects of His being. But do not take up permanent residence in the low-lying communities of the borderlands. *Live among the mountaintops.*

In all things, at all times, in every circumstance...*call Him Father!*

Abba is the heart's cry of intimacy. Truly, He is a God to call Father.

ABBA IS THE HEART'S CRY OF INTIMACY. TRULY, HE IS A GOD TO CALL FATHER.

Our Father, we cannot adequately express to You our deep gratitude for what You have revealed to us about Yourself. O God, reveal yet more! Open us to the fullness with which You desire that we see You. How can we possibly thank You for being so good, so loving, so trustworthy, so forgiving toward us, and toward all the sons and daughters of Your creation? In truth, there is only one way, by entering all the more fully into Your Fatherhood, which has been our destiny from the beginning.

Fill the reservoirs within us with the waters of Your being! Keep those waters fresh and life-giving by the continually renewed immediacy of Your presence.

Help us, Father. We are yet so small in our thinking, so blind to the magnitude of Your love, so tentative in our trust, so fearful of what Your goodness might mean, so reluctant to recognize the extent to which Your forgiveness extends.

Oh, but it is the deepest desire of our hearts to walk in increased intimacy with You! Help us, we pray. Draw us, nurture us, guide our steps, keep hold of our hands, and lead us further into that unbounded chamber of intimacy we desire but are too small to apprehend.

Let us rejoice in our childness, and seek it all the more, leaving behind the independence of the world and entering into the divine childlikeness shown us by Jesus and that made Him our Savior. Whatever is required, transform us into sons and daughters who reflect the image of Your Son.

Reveal Yourself to us, we ask again. Open our eyes to see You where Your holy being shouts with divine silence. Guide our steps now, as we continue into the innermost regions of Your heart which know no end.

Thank You, Father, that we can make Your heart our home.

Thank You, above all, that we have learned to call You Father.

Exciting titles
by Don Nori

NO MORE SOUR GRAPES

Who among us wants our children to be free from the struggles we have had to bear? Who among us wants the lives of our children to be full of victory and love for their Lord? Who among us wants the hard-earned lessons from our lives given freely to our children? All these are not only possible, they are also God's will. You can be one of those who share the excitement and joy of seeing your children step into the destiny God has for them. If you answered "yes" to these questions, the pages of this book are full of hope and help for you and others just like you.
ISBN 0-7684-2037-7

THE POWER OF BROKENNESS

Accepting Brokenness is a must for becoming a true vessel of the Lord, and is a stepping-stone to revival in our hearts, our homes, and our churches. Brokenness alone brings us to the wonderful revelation of how deep and great our Lord's mercy really is. Join this companion who leads us through the darkest of nights. Discover the *Power of Brokenness*.
ISBN 1-56043-178-4

THE ANGEL AND THE JUDGMENT

Few understand the power of our judgments—or the aftermath of the words we speak in thoughtless, emotional pain. In this powerful story about a preacher and an angel, you'll see how the heavens respond and how the earth is changed by the words we utter in secret.
ISBN 1-56043-154-7

HIS MANIFEST PRESENCE

This is a passionate look at God's desire for a people with whom He can have intimate fellowship. Not simply a book on worship, it faces our triumphs as well as our sorrows in relation to God's plan for a dwelling place that is splendid in holiness and love.
ISBN 0-914903-48-9
Also available in Spanish.
ISBN 1-56043-079-6

SECRETS OF THE MOST HOLY PLACE

Here is a prophetic parable you will read again and again. The winds of God are blowing, drawing you to His Life within the Veil of the Most Holy Place. There you begin to see as you experience a depth of relationship your heart has yearned for. This book is a living, dynamic experience with God!
ISBN 1-56043-076-1

HOW TO FIND GOD'S LOVE

Here is a heartwarming story about three people who tell their stories of tragedy, fear, and disease, and how God showed them His love in a real way.
ISBN 0-914903-28-4
Also available in Spanish.
ISBN 1-56043-024-9

Available at your local Christian bookstore.

6B-1:15

Foundationally Spirit-filled. Biblically Sound. Spiritually Inspirational.

FROM THE FATHER'S HEART
by Charles Slagle.
This is a beautiful look at the true heart of your heavenly Father. Through these sensitive selections that include short love notes, letters, and prophetic words from God to His children, you will develop the kind of closeness and intimacy with the loving Father that you have always longed for. From words of encouragement and inspiration to words of gentle correction, each letter addresses times that we all experience. For those who diligently seek God, you will recognize Him in these pages.
ISBN 0-914903-82-9

AN INVITATION TO FRIENDSHIP:
From the Father's Heart, Volume 2
by Charles Slagle.
Our God is a Father whose heart longs for His children to sit and talk with Him in fellowship and oneness. This second volume of intimate letters from the Father to you, His child, reveals His passion, dreams, and love for you. As you read them, you will find yourself drawn ever closer within the circle of His embrace. The touch of His presence will change your life forever!
ISBN 0-7684-2013-X

THE ASCENDED LIFE
by Bernita J. Conway.
A believer does not need to wait until Heaven to experience an intimate relationship with the Lord. When you are born again, your life becomes His, and He pours His life into yours. Here Bernita Conway explains from personal study and experience the truth of "abiding in the Vine," the Lord Jesus Christ. When you grasp this understanding and begin to walk in it, it will change your whole life and relationship with your heavenly Father!
ISBN 1-56043-337-X

TODAY GOD IS FIRST
by Os Hillman.
Sometimes it is hard to keep Him first in my day. It is a struggle to see Him in the circumstances of my job. I need help to bring the reality of my Lord into my place of work. Os Hillman has the uncanny ability to write just to my circumstance, exactly to my need. He helps me see God's view. He strengthens my faith and courage to both see God and invite Him into the everyday trials and struggles of work. Take this book to work, put it on your desk or table. Every day just before you tackle the mountains before you, pause long enough to remind yourself—Today, God Is First.
ISBN 0-7684-2049-0

Available at your local Christian bookstore.

For more information and sample chapters, visit www.destinyimage.com

6B-2:86

Books to help you grow strong in Jesus

➤ ## WORSHIP AS DAVID LIVED IT

by Judson Cornwall.

This book about David's heart and life as a worshiper will show you the intimacy and the necessity of God's nearness as it is discovered in a life of worship.

ISBN 1-56043-700-6

➤ ## DAVID WORSHIPED WITH A FERVENT FAITH

by Judson Cornwall.

David had a joyful faith given him by God, and he applied that faith consistently to the circumstances of life. Journey with David through his psalms and you will uncover a fervent faith that is relevant for you today!

ISBN 1-56043-089-3

➤ ## DAVID WORSHIPED A LIVING GOD

by Judson Cornwall.

Jehovah Rapha, Jehovah Shalom, Jehovah Shammah, Jehovah Jireh—King David knew his God by these names and more. Learn what each name means. Discover how the Almighty can reveal Himself to you through each attribute.

ISBN 0-938612-38-7

➤ ## RESTORING THE DANCE

by Ann Stevenson.

Can we dance in our worship to the Lord? Why has dancing in the Church been "on trial" for so long? Why is dance now being restored to the Church? Today God is unfolding His plan for dance in His house. In *Restoring the Dance* Ann Stevenson teaches the scriptural foundation for dance in worship. As a mature dancer in the Lord and founder of a large Christian dance troupe, she demonstrates the need for dance in our Father's House.

ISBN 1-56043-305-1

Available at your local Christian bookstore.

For more information and sample chapters, visit www.destinyimage.com

6B-1:21

Classic titles
from Destiny Image

━ THE ACCEPTABLE SACRIFICE
by John Bunyan.

John Bunyan's words are delivered with compelling conviction as he passionately portrays the beauty of the only sacrifice that is acceptable to God. With carefully crafted words he describes the wonder and majesty of a heart broken before the Lord. The brokenhearted are not forsaken or ignored, for they are "His jewels, His beloved." *The Acceptable Sacrifice* is a timeless message and must be read by all who desire to enter into the Presence of the Lord.
ISBN: 0-7684-5004-7

━ NO CROSS, NO CROWN
by William Penn.

While in a London prison in 1668, William Penn wrote *No Cross, No Crown*. His most famous work, it is a discourse on the power of the cross and self-denial. In dramatic and persuasive style Penn portrays the beauty and power of the cross as the only pathway to the crown. "Christ's cross, is Christ's way to Christ's crown." Penn's great passion was that this book would win the heart of man for his beloved Master.
ISBN: 0-9707919-1-7

Available at your local Christian bookstore.

For more information and sample chapters, visit www.destinyimage.com

6B-2:78